feng shui

for personal harmony

feng shui

for personal harmony

Gary Khor

SIMON & SCHUSTER

AUSTRALIA

First published in Australia in 2000 by
Simon & Schuster (Australia) Pty Limited
20 Barcoo Street,
East Roseville NSW 2069

A Viacom Company
Sydney New York London Toronto Tokyo Singapore

National Library of Australia
Cataloguing-in-Publication Data

Khor, Gary, 1947– .
    Feng shui for personal harmony.

    Bibliography.
    Includes index.
    ISBN 0 7318 0923 8.

    1. Feng-shui. I. Title.

133.3337

Set in Sabon 11/14pt
Cover and text design by Greendot Design
Typeset by Midland Typesetters
Illustrations by Lorenzo Lucia
Printed in Australia by Griffin

10 9 8 7 6 5 4 3 2 1

Contents

What is Feng Shui?   7

Chapter 1
Introducing Feng Shui —The Art of Making Life 'Click'   9

Chapter 2
Creating a Personal Energy Profile —
Identifying Your Environmental Energy Needs   31

Chapter 3
Creating an Environmental Energy Profile —
Building a Picture of Your Environment   61

Chapter 4
The Positive Feng Shui Program in Action   97

Chapter 5
Developing Your Feng Shui Skills   177

Index   221

What is Feng Shui?

Feng Shui is the art of analysing and understanding your immediate environment, and changing your surroundings to generate optimum conditions in which to thrive. Enhancement of your surroundings can increase your potential for health, success, prosperity and happiness.

To the Chinese, having good Feng Shui means leading a charmed life. That is, to lead a 'smoothly flowing' life, with everything you touch turning out right; everything 'clicks'. In the West we would call this 'having the Midas touch'.

The Chinese see the whole universe as one unified energy system, with each human being, although a singular enclosed energy unit, also interacting directly with this larger energy system. Therefore, for each of us to function at our best, we must be in total harmony, both within ourselves and with our surrounding environment.

With this concept in mind, and utilising the principles of yin and yang, the five elements theory and the earth's energy flow, the Chinese created Feng Shui as a means of harmonising their lives with their immediate environments and with nature as a whole.

Over the years, the art of Feng Shui has encompassed rational and scientific facts, psychology, cultural beliefs, intuition, and also superstition. This book sets out to explain all of these various factors to help you to separate fact from superstition and thus utilise Feng Shui to improve your life.

Chapter 1

Introducing Feng Shui —
The Art Of Making Life 'Click'

Why practise Feng Shui?

There are times in life when everything seems to 'click' into place. We feel healthy and vibrant; the things we do are successful and rewarding; we have sufficient money to live the type of life we want; we feel well-balanced and harmonious; we feel happy! We often set ourselves goals, such as saving so much money, earning so much income, gaining such and such a degree, maybe even having a certain number of children. But, in essence, all of these things are simply a means to an end — happiness.

There are very few people who would not, in their hearts, want to make themselves and their families happier, or even make the world itself a happier place. Perhaps the greatest tragedy is that so many people simply dismiss such objectives as being beyond reach. However, in reality we can either move towards a more happy state of mind, or further away from it.

The Chinese quest — a long life with health, prosperity and success

For millennia, the Chinese have focused on the pursuit of a 'happy' existence, so much so that in Chinese homes and businesses you will often see the three statues representing 'Wealth', 'Happiness' and

THE THREE CHINESE STATUES

Longevity   Success   Wealth

'Longevity' that symbolise this quest. The Chinese also pondered the question of what makes everything 'click'. Is it just chance or fate (the will of the gods), or can we do something about it?

The traditional Chinese people did not eliminate luck, destiny or the will of the gods as significant players in individuals' lives but they did identify two areas where people were able to improve their chances of making things 'click'. First, like members of other cultures, the Chinese realised that if you were not going to rely on uncontrollable elements such as luck or divine influence to make things fall your way, then you needed to invest some personal effort — both mentally and physically — in your life and community.

Second, and this is where the Chinese differed from other cultures, they noticed that the nature of one's personal environment and surroundings was associated with one's chances of finding the 'click'. Thus, selection of that environment, together with identification of beneficial elements and modification of those that were not, increased those chances. These techniques became known as Feng Shui.

Feng Shui is not magic, nor is it an appeal to the supernatural. It is an understanding of the natural forces of the universe and of ourselves, and of how interactions between the two can be used to move us in the direction of happiness (or the 'click'). Practising Feng Shui does not guarantee perfect happiness but, if understood and used properly, it can increase your current level of happiness.

Happiness might seem a vague objective (though not so vague that the founders of the American constitution did not see fit to enshrine its 'pursuit' as the inalienable right of every individual) but the model developed by the Chinese, the eight major life energies, provides ways to balance and harmonise all the aspects of your life, which, in turn, contribute to that overall state. Feng Shui techniques are not limited to improving the happiness of individuals but apply equally to families, groups, businesses and organisations (see Note 9 on pages 201–3).

 The Chinese ideograms for Feng Shui literally translate as wind and water. Wind symbolises the movement and dispersal of energy; water symbolises the gathering of energy.

The essence of Feng Shui

The essence of Feng Shui is simple:
• The environment contains energy (or, more accurately, *is* energy).
• This energy affects living things (including human beings).
• Our environment can be changed or modified to make its effects more beneficial.

Just as different diets or exercise programs are appropriate for different individuals, so each individual does better within some energetic environments than they do in others. Feng Shui is therefore the art of identifying the individual's energy needs, and selecting or adjusting an environment in order to provide them.

Did you know that you already practise Feng Shui?

Each and every one of us already practises some degree of Feng Shui in the way we manage the energy of our environment. We use heaters

11

in the winter, fans and airconditioners in the summer, lights when it's dark, etc. When we do these things, we are adjusting the energy of our environment. Even such basic activities as flicking a switch on an electrical appliance makes changes to environmental energy that can have profound effects on our lives.

When we control energies such as heat, light and sound in our environment we do not just make ourselves more comfortable, but potentially we:

- **improve our health** – whose health does well in a cold, damp, draughty environment?
- **improve our productivity and creativity** – who studies or works well in a loud, noisy environment?
- **improve our relationships** – there are some relationship activities that just don't proceed well when you are freezing, or feeling faint from the heat!

When we are healthier, when we are more productive, when we maintain better relationships (not only with family and friends but with workmates and colleagues), should we be surprised if we are happier and more content?

So far, we have only mentioned energy effects of the environment that are so obvious that we almost don't have to think about them. But there's the danger! Many of us in the West have stopped thinking about the environment; we have relied on our automatic responses to get us through. The traditional Chinese took another approach in their search for the 'click', or for having a smoothly flowing life filled with successful undertakings. They studied their environment and surroundings, day after day, century after century, millennia after millennia, looking for clues. What energy affected people in what ways? How could energetic effects be detected or predicted? What could be done about them? Thus, the art of Feng Shui was born.

Where are the dragons?

'Whoa!' I can almost hear you say. 'This all sounds very commonsense and matter of fact. Isn't Feng Shui about mountains and rivers, about locating white tigers and green dragons, about dragon veins, compass directions and strange astrological and numerological calculations?'

It is very important that we do not confuse the objectives of Feng Shui (making us happier) with the various techniques used. The techniques all have a common purpose in that they enable us to gather more information about our environment — what its effects on us will be and how we can make positive adjustments to it. As such, they are only tools; the important thing is what we achieve with them. We also need to remember that the words and images are taken from a different culture and era, and often simply reflect the only words and imagery available at that time. If the same concepts are to be successfully communicated in a different era and culture, those words and images may need to be reinterpreted.

If you have a more mystical disposition, you can see environmental energy as having the nature of dragons and tigers. If you have a scientific disposition, then you may see Feng Shui purely in terms of physical energy interactions. The Feng Shui will still work, whatever imagery you use.

Consider the West's adoption of the word 'acupuncture'. A Western doctor giving acupuncture will explain some of its effects in terms of nerve gate theory (that acupuncture works on the nervous, rather than the energetic, system) and the release of endorphins. The same treatment from a Chinese doctor will include an explanation couched in terms of energy balancing. However, does it make any difference which explanation is used, as long as you are cured? Just as acupuncture works, however it is explained, so does Feng Shui.

It is not the intention of this book to rationalise or demysticise Feng Shui. Rather, the aim is to show that there is a whole range of approaches to it — that as long as you accept the fundamental premise, you can choose the most comfortable approach. I call this range of approaches the 'Feng Shui spectrum'. You can limit yourself to the scientific and rational, or you can have all the dragons and tigers you desire. The only thing I am interested in is ensuring Feng Shui works for you. (In saying this, I do not mean to suggest that the scientific approach is a dry and colourless one. The universe is such a wonderful and amazing place that scientific facts have their own magic!)

The Feng Shui spectrum is not just the choice between science and dragons. There is a whole range of approaches, encompassing those of a scientific, psychological, cultural, mystic or even downright superstitious nature. While you can discard those approaches with which you are uncomfortable, remember they are all basically approaches for gathering and evaluating information about your environment, and that the more information and perspectives you can get, the better. However, you need to understand a little more about each of these approaches before you commit yourself to the approach(es) you are going to use.

The spectrum of Feng Shui techniques

COMMON SENSE	RATIONAL AND SCIENTIFIC i.e. physical and tangible	PSYCHO-LOGICAL (mind)	UNKNOWN/ INTUITIVE Temporary acceptance while being researched	CULTURAL BELIEFS e.g. Chinese number 4 = death or bad luck	SUPERSTITION Old wives' tales or unsubstantiated stories
AFFECTS ALL				SECTION OF POPULATION ONLY — RACE	UNEDUCATED/ GULLIBLE

Common sense approach
If an environment is too cold, we warm it; if it is too dark, we lighten it; if we reduce the number of sharp, spiky objects in an environment, we create a safer, more comfortable one. It is obvious that, we improve our chances of happiness and security when we do not build our homes on steep, unstable slopes or on the side of an active volcano! Many of the actions recommended in this book have this commonsense element.

Scientific approach
This concerns things that may not be obvious, but have been established as facts through observation and experimentation. It is known, for instance, that exposure to full-spectrum instead of fluorescent lighting *keeps* individuals healthier and more productive.

Our bodies evolved in natural sunlight, and as a consequence only function at their best in an environment that has light of similar wavelengths to that found in natural sunlight. We can use such scientific knowledge to decide which information to collect about our environment, how to interpret the effects of our environment and how to adjust our environment optimally.

Psychological approach

Let's say that someone who is seeking to improve their career prospects becomes focused on making changes to their environment to assist with this. We could say that making these changes has an element of positive affirmation that will enable the person to become more confident, and thus see and take advantage of opportunities in their workplace, which then improves their career prospects.

The unknown

There are certain approaches to Feng Shui that are based on apparently logical assumptions, as yet unproven by science. But, then again, much is still unexplained by science, and many things that exist today, for example, mobile phones and surgical transplants, started out as science fiction (or, in earlier cultures, magic). Sometimes it is enough that things work without us knowing why they do! We just have to accept that we do not yet know everything, and that hopefully more things will become clear.

Cultural approach

Each culture has certain customs and beliefs which work within it. For instance, if one Aborigine 'points the bone' at another, the other Aborigine may die; if the bone were pointed at someone of another culture, that person may well walk away laughing. For the members of a culture, that culture's customs and beliefs can have very real effects.

Superstitious approach

Superstition refers to associations and beliefs that have developed within a culture but are not accepted by the majority of the members of that culture as valid beliefs. For instance, most Westerners would probably be unconcerned at having No. 13 as an address, but some may be convinced that terrible things would happen to them. A superstitious Chinese person would be worried about living at No. 4 (in Chinese, the words for 'four' and 'death' sound the same). Local superstitions may have significance for those who believe them, but when practising Feng Shui we should ignore other cultures' superstitions which have no meaning for us.

This book's approach

This book has an approach that is primarily at the common sense, scientific end of the Feng Shui spectrum but, rather than rejecting other, 'as yet unproven', aspects, it accepts them where they seem to work. In doing this, I make use of my experience in the study of chi in the internal arts (exercise, meditation, massage, etc.), knowing that these arts function quite well without necessarily incorporating mysticism or spiritual aspects. (Please note that the above statement uses the words 'without *necessarily* incorporating'. Internal chi arts *can* make use of mystic and spiritual techniques, and, perhaps, can then result in more success and higher-quality lives for their practitioners. However, it is a matter of individual choice.)

Getting the traditional Chinese perspective

While it is probably easy for you to understand that the energy in the environment can affect us, this is not really the traditional Chinese perspective. To the Chinese, energy isn't just *in* the environment, it *is* the environment! Modern science would tend to agree.

To make it apparent how the Western 'matter'-orientated view of the environment distorts our perception of reality, when I am giving workshops I will often hold up a four-sided box with no top and no bottom, and ask the audience to tell me what is inside. Inevitably, the first answer is 'Nothing'. When I reject this and the audience does a little more thinking, the next answer is usually 'Air'. I then point out the following:

- The audience can see me through the open box, so there is light energy in there.
- The audience can hear me when I speak from the other side of the box, so there is sound energy in there.
- When I put my hand in the box it does not freeze, so there is thermal energy in there.

- When I release an object such as a pencil in the box, it falls, so there is gravitational energy there.
- When I place a compass in the box it points north, so there is magnetic energy there.
- When I place a transistor radio in the box it plays music, so there are radio waves in there.

There are many other examples that I could use but, by this time, the audience is starting to get the point.

We live in an ocean of energy; there is no such thing as an empty room, or empty anything. The so-called vacuum that scientists create is no vacuum as far as energy is concerned. We sometimes talk of fish being so conditioned to their water environment that they do not notice it. Well, how often do you think of the ocean of energy in which you live?

Instead of seeing your environment as space filled with the occasional lump of matter, see matter itself as just another form of energy in an energetic ocean. When you make this change in perspective, it becomes obvious why you should be as concerned about the quality of energy in which you live as you are about the quality of air you breathe.

The analogy of the ocean is a good one because, just as water oceans have currents and tides, so too does the energetic ocean. Some currents are of cool energy, others of warm energy. Some currents are rich and nutritious, supporting life; other currents are empty and barren. There are few people who have stood at the edge of a water ocean and not been awed by its beauty and power. When you see your whole environment as an energetic ocean these feelings become magnified, because we don't stand on the edge of this ocean, we live in its depths.

What is energy?

Having got to the point where we can see our environment as an ocean of energy, we now have to understand what the Chinese have learnt about energy during their millennia of study. In the Western 'matter'-dominated world, gold and iron look and act differently, yet they are composed of identical protons, neutrons and electrons — the only difference being the number of protons, neutrons and electrons that make up the atoms has changed. It was in the explosion of stars that all the different types of atoms that make up our bodies were formed. Very basically, human beings, along with everything around us, are just transmuted hydrogen atoms.

In a similar manner, the Chinese see all the various energies around us as 'transmutations' of the basic energy that they call 'chi'. Just as the same subatomic particles, in different arrangements, have the soft feel of the fur of animals or the crystalline beauty of a sparkling diamond, so it is chi energy that underlies the golden glow of sunset, the warmth of a human hand or the melodious sound of a babbling brook. Light, sound, heat, magnetism, gravity, microwaves, and all the other energies we see around us, are just different aspects of chi.

This recognition of the make-up of energy is as fundamental to the Chinese understanding of the universe as subatomic theory is to Western understanding, and for largely the same reasons. Subatomic particles obey certain laws no matter what element or atom they are in. So, too, chi obeys certain laws, no matter what type of energy it manifests itself as.

This knowledge is fundamental to Feng Shui, allowing us to predict the effects environmental energy has on us and to make changes to the environment that will change those effects in predictable ways. It also explains why you can't get far with Feng Shui without understanding a little about chi. This is why chi, and how it behaves, is the beginning of our journey into Feng Shui. We know the destination of our journey (the 'click') and we know our route (through the ocean of chi), but now we must learn a little about the vessel that will carry us — the positive Feng Shui program.

The positive Feng Shui program

Most people do Feng Shui for the same reason that they exercise or diet: for the benefits these practices bring. Few people who diet or exercise want to study to become a nutritionist or a physiotherapist; they only want a basic understanding of these fields and guidance in what to do. The positive Feng Shui program (in future, just referred to as 'the program') provides just such understanding and guidance.

The program focuses on simple, inexpensive techniques that

provide the means of improving the energetic environment of your home and work environment, and getting that 'click'. Rather than having to wade through a mountain of theory, it gets you up and running with Feng Shui right away. It puts *you* in charge of *your* Feng Shui.

This program seeks to avoid a 'negative' approach to Feng Shui. By negative I mean an approach similar to the old approach to health which saw health merely as 'the absence of sickness'. In this approach, if a sickness could not be found, the person was proclaimed healthy, completely missing the point that health is a positive state of vibrant wellbeing, not just the absence of the flu! A problem-focussed negative approach to Feng Shui makes it about as much fun as going for a medical check-up! This program focuses you on improving your happiness and quality of life, not on seeking out problems in your environment.

So in this program it is the 'click' that we are aiming for, not the 'absence of problems'. Human life is not about the absence of misery, it is about fulfilment and happiness. This should be our aim in practising Feng Shui.

Some more thoughts on the importance of staying positive

Positive Feng Shui reflects an important approach to life. That is, go looking for problems in your life and you will find them. Go looking for improvements and opportunities, and you will find them too. Likewise, the attitude you have towards Feng Shui will affect what you get out of the practice.

Let's imagine a person who, on waking each morning, repeats one hundred times, 'I will not get sick.' It's a pretty safe bet that it won't be too long before that person gets sick! Why? Because of the role of the subconscious.

We can better understand how the subconscious works by considering advertising. Advertisers certainly know what they are doing. All of us like to think we are immune to the tricks of advertisers (it's only those *other* sheep who get sucked in!). The fact is that those tens of billions of advertising dollars spent every year continue to get spent because advertisements work. They work because they are based on a very sound appreciation of how the mind operates.

If we understand what advertisers do, we can use these same principles for our own benefit.

Advertisers work by slipping 'images' past the 'conscious censor' into the subconscious (which has a lot more say in what we buy and do than most of us would like to think). Advertisers know that the subconscious is actually that, *sub*conscious. It does not understand speech, it cannot read, it simply picks up the images held by the conscious mind when it listens, reads or otherwise interprets sensory input.

For example, you don't have to have an IQ of 160 to know that smoking is not only unhealthy but an unattractive habit. So, if you're an advertiser trying to sell a product that no conscious mind would entertain buying, you don't sell it to the conscious mind, you sell it to the subconscious. To do this, you get the subconscious used to seeing the images of healthy, attractive people associated with the images of smoking. How readily the subconscious accepts this, and whether it is the conscious or subconscious mind that calls the shots, is demonstrated quite powerfully by the hundreds of thousands who die each year of lung cancer caused by smoking. (Of course, smoking has started to decline in our society since the anti-smoking lobby started getting *its* images across to the subconscious.)

Don't blame the subconscious for this subversion. As humankind evolved, it made a lot of sense that human beings should be positively motivated to do the sort of things they saw being done by healthy, attractive, successful members of their species. (After all, perhaps that's what made them healthy, attractive and successful!) It's just that some devious conscious minds use advertising to associate images falsely with other things, misleading the subconscious and thereby slipping information past conscious brains they would otherwise have been unable to fool directly.

To return to our original example, if what you seek is health, then to keep saying to yourself 'I will not get sick' is counterproductive. The only image that impinges on the subconscious is the image of being sick. So keep bringing that image up often enough and that is what you will become. If you want health rather than sickness, the image your conscious mind needs to have is one of health. (In many ways, it is actually quite marvellous that our mind and body only function correctly when our thoughts are happy, vital and positive. Just consider how appalling the alternative would be!)

Now, let's apply the same logic to our 'image' of the environment. If all we see around us are 'daggers' of energy and evil influences, an environment out to 'get us', then we are placing very negative and disturbing influences in our subconscious mind. Should we be surprised if this 'image' results in stress and tension, if our energy is lowered and immune system compromised? As our health deteriorates and, along with it, the energy that we have to put into career and relationships wanes, should we expect the quality of our lives to improve or worsen? Will we move closer to the 'click', or further from it?

It is much better to learn to look at your environment positively — not to look for threats but for opportunities, and to think about how you can improve things, about what could be even better. This program is about giving you that positive mental framework and allowing you to use Feng Shui in a constructive, rather than destructive, way.

How much do you need to know?

The good news is that to carry out the program there is much that is *interesting* to know, but very little that you *have* to know. The techniques and approaches detailed in the program work whether or not you understand the more detailed aspects of Feng Shui (in the same way that you don't need to know much about electricity to be able to use it in your day-to-day life).

The basic background knowledge is found in Chapter 2; more detailed knowledge in Chapter 5. As you progress through the text you will be alerted to the existence of relevant notes in Chapter 5, to which you can then refer if you wish to do so.

Primarily, these notes have been included to show that there is a logical and consistent basis to Feng Shui. Nonetheless, in a similar manner to Western science, Feng Shui contains differing viewpoints and alternate theories, and some of the notes provide outlines of the arguments that are used to support the various opinions. (Beware of practitioners who tell you that Feng Shui was magically revealed in its entirety some 5000 years ago. This is generally a cover to stop you asking questions that the practitioner cannot answer! As these people do not even know the history of their own subject, it's unlikely they will know too much else.)

Getting the most out of the program

While the program can be used on its own to improve quality of life, it is only one of the chi 'living skills' developed by the traditional Chinese. The more of these chi living skills you use, the better the overall result will tend to be.

A good analogy is that of a person working on their health. While spending a certain number of hours exercising each week will deliver benefits, if you keep increasing the number of hours you will eventually reach the point of diminishing return. More and more effort is then required to get small, incremental improvements in health. Much better results would be obtained by the person putting this extra effort into improving other aspects of their life, such as diet, rest and mental focus.

This program is designed to be used the same way that the traditional Chinese used Feng Shui — as one part of a balanced approach to life. (Refer to Note 1 on pages 178–9 for a brief introduction to the chi living skills and how they can be used in combination with the positive Feng Shui program.)

Dispelling some common Feng Shui myths

Feng Shui consultants are like any other cross-section of society — you will find the good, the bad and the ugly. The majority have the interests of their clients at heart but it has not escaped the notice of others that, if they can appeal to fear and greed in the human character, and convince their victims that only they have the skills and 'secret formula' to save or to enrich the victim, there's the odd dollar to be made. Because of this, a number of Feng Shui myths have grown up which need to be dispelled.

- **Feng Shui is not about making millions.** It is about creating a balanced, happy life. The proportion of Feng Shui consultant millionaires is not statistically different to the rest of the population. (Also, if your Feng Shui consultant does not seem happy and balanced, ponder how their skills will work for you if they don't work for them!)

- **There are no dark and sinister Feng Shui forces out to get you.** These forces do not exist any more than there are automobiles out to get you (but it never hurts to look both ways when you cross the road!).
- **If your house faces north, south, east, or whatever, you are not doomed to a life of poverty and degradation.** However, if you want to build a home on the slopes of an active volcano, don't be surprised to find you have more excitement in your life than you may want!

Common (and not so common) questions about Feng Shui

Those impatient to get to it and start managing their own Feng Shui could proceed directly to Chapter 2. The section you are reading now has been included simply to answer some common questions asked in Feng Shui and provide a little of the 'flavour' of Feng Shui.

Do I have to own a house or business premises to have Feng Shui?
No. It is not the ownership of buildings that is important, so it is irrelevant to your Feng Shui whether you own, lease or squat in the property in which you live or work. The energy simply interacts with the energies of whomever comes within its range of influence. Therefore, you do not have to own a property for its Feng Shui to affect you; it is where you spend your time that is important.

However, while the energy of an environment does not act of its own volition, you do. This means that the 'relationship' you have with the property can have both direct and indirect effects on the energy of the building and the way this interacts with your personal energy. For instance, if you don't like the place you live in, not only are you likely to spend less time within its influence but you are likely to be less in tune with its energy. Thus, you are less liable to make the day-to-day changes that even people totally oblivious to Feng Shui make to improve the quality of their environment.

What is most important for my Feng Shui: the house I live in or the building I work in?

Feng Shui arises from the influence of the energy of the environment in which you live and work on your personal energy. In general terms, the more time we spend in an environment the greater the influence it will have on our Feng Shui, and the more attention we should pay to it to make sure that the energy is as good as it can be.

The other factor to be taken into account is the nature of activity that takes place in a particular environment. For instance, if you own your own business, the Feng Shui of the property in which you carry out that business will probably influence your work more than the place where you live. Likewise, the Feng Shui of your home will probably have more influence on your family relationships than will the place where you work. We have to use the word 'probably' because lifestyles vary so much. If you are on the road most of the year, then the home that you infrequently return to will not have as strong an influence as it would on someone who lives and works from their home.

If you want to work on improving relationships through Feng Shui, then you need to consider where activity connected with the relationship occurs. For instance, if you are travelling a lot, then the types of environments from where you choose to telephone your partner can be important. Bear in mind that relationships involve more than one person and that even though one partner may be away from the home, the fact that the other partner resides there means the Feng Shui of the home still has a strong influence on the relationship. If both parties are away from the home much of the time, then its influence on relationships will be minimal.

If study, sporting and social activities consume significant portions of your time and so are important elements of your life, don't overlook the influence of places where you engage in these activities.

When a business is carried on in a building, who gets that building's Feng Shui — the building owner, the business owner, the business itself or the people who work in the building?

From the answers above, we know that unless the building owner actually spends a significant portion of time at the building, their Feng Shui is not going to be affected by it. Likewise, the business owner must be at the premises to be affected. As for publicly listed companies, it is the shareholders who own the assets, including the buildings. Should you own shares in a company, your Feng Shui will not be directly affected by the various buildings the company may own or operate from. (However, the Feng Shui of the premises will influence the fortunes of the company, which will then have an impact on the value of your investment!)

A business is an activity (businesses that don't do anything generally aren't very successful!). The energy of this activity will be affected by the energy of the environment in which the business operates. So, businesses do have Feng Shui, as do hospitals, education facilities, sporting venues, clubs and so on.

The Feng Shui for business buildings relates to the activities that are carried on in them. The energy which supports management and strategic thinking — as may occur at a head office — can be quite different to that needed for retail or manufacturing activities, and it may well be advantageous to have different locations for each department — head office, research and development, marketing, etc. If you can't have separate buildings you can still create separate environments by using colour and furnishings. For example, a marketing department should not have the same decor as a legal department, and vice versa.

It should come as no surprise that the people who work in a building will have their personal Feng Shui affected. The strongest influence will be on their careers but there will also be influences on all other areas of their lives.

Can a tent or caravan, boats, cars and planes have Feng Shui?

Asking if a tent or caravan can have Feng Shui is another way of asking the question, 'Do bigger houses have better Feng Shui?' The answer is: not in themselves. Buildings have the effect of modifying the energy of the local environment. If the energy in a location is poor to begin with, then, even if you build a palace there, the Feng Shui is not likely to be much good. On the other hand, some locations have very good energy, so even shacks or tents erected in them, or caravans parked in them, can provide beneficial environments for their inhabitants. (Many successful Chinese businesspeople continue to live in houses that they started out in, due to fear of losing the good Feng Shui that made them successful.)

That said, it has to be acknowledged that for any specific location the more the building constructed at that location is able to support a positive energy environment, the better the Feng Shui will be. That is, a building cannot of itself *create* good Feng Shui but it can fail to *maintain* it. Equally, we can state that a general rule for real estate and Feng Shui is that a poor house in an excellent position is preferable to an excellent house in a poor position. It is easier to do something about the house than about the house's position.

Let's use cooking as an analogy. If the food being cooked has little or no nutritional value, then, while cooking might make the food *look* better, it cannot actually add nutritional value to it. On the other hand, if the food had excellent nutritional value originally but was cooked poorly, this could render the food nutritionally valueless. Similarly, if you live in a dwelling of such poor construction or which is so poorly maintained that it cannot be properly heated or cooled, or the premises leak, making them damp and cold, it is unlikely that the Feng Shui will be much good, however good the energy of the local environment was to begin with.

If you live in a tent or caravan and move around a lot, then you can't rely on your abode maintaining the quality of the environmental energy. You must therefore pay more attention than most to the condition of your environmental energy and how to enhance it.

Boats, cars and planes all move around, but they still exist in a particular environment and will therefore be modifying the energy of that environment. Those people who spend substantial parts of their lives in moving vehicles, particularly when they eat and sleep in them on a regular basis, need to consider the Feng Shui aspects of those vehicles.

People who live, for example, on houseboats and yachts, and in mobile caravans, are constantly changing the direction in which these abodes face. Feng Shui in respect of compass directions is totally impracticable, and is another reason that I consider compass directions in themselves play a relatively small role in Feng Shui.

Can Feng Shui be 'used up'?

The energy of your environment will influence your Feng Shui without being 'used up'. Think of a magnetic field: when you let a magnet attract a piece of metal, you don't use up part of the magnet. Likewise, when a meteorite is pulled down to the surface of the earth, it does not use up part of the earth's gravitational field. (Actually, it ends up strengthening the field because of the addition of mass!) Thus, when we build a new house, we don't build into it Feng Shui that gets gradually used up. The reverse is often the case, with the Feng Shui of well-maintained older houses that have accumulated positive experiences actually being more beneficial.

This does *not* mean that the Feng Shui, or energy, of an environment cannot be degraded. All nature changes. The energy flows in an environment are continually changing, sometimes increasing in strength and sometimes decreasing. When occurring naturally, this is *generally* a slow process (although not always; major geological and meteorological events can change Feng Shui quickly, but such events are the exception rather than the rule.) In today's world, the most likely cause of changes in the chi energy of the environment are the actions of humanity. Major construction or change in your local environment, such as when a rural area becomes a suburb, or a desert area is irrigated, can introduce major change quite quickly.

While Feng Shui isn't *used up*, one does need to take account of the fact that people, as well as environments around them, will change. The nature of the supporting environments that people need may thus change over their lifetimes. You will often find that, after years of being content in one location, people suddenly feel the need to change it. Often this is rationalised as having different housing requirements but most times they could have modified their original houses for less than it cost them to move to their new ones. If a person *has* lived a long time in one place, it is not unusual for them to change little in their character and activities over the years.

Should astronauts worry about Feng Shui?

This is not a frivolous question, for a number of reasons. Space Station Freedom, the new international space station, will be the most expensive construction ever built; it would be a shame if it had bad Feng Shui! Once we start building interplanetary constructions (and, who knows, in future people may live for substantial periods or even their entire lives on such constructions) we will have to come to grips with the universal aspects of Feng Shui.

By its very definition, chi is universal, and wherever we go in this universe its energy is going to influence our own. However, when you're drifting around in interstellar space, compass directions don't have too much significance. Likewise, to the first person born on Mars (or elsewhere in space), it's not going to make much difference whether it was the Year of the Rat, or whatever, on earth. Universal time does not exist, as time passes differently depending on the speed being travelled at. If a galaxy, solar system or planet, etc., happens to be travelling at a fair portion of the speed of light, then the speed at which time passes is going to be unique to its inhabitants (and everything else travelling at that same speed).

It's not being suggested that times and directions are not important; rather that they reflect some deeper aspect of chi energy not fully explained by compass direction and earth dating systems. A particular relationship, workable on earth but actually reflective of a deeper principle, may express itself as a quite different relationship elsewhere. (This is not all academic; it has already arisen in applying relationships learnt in the Northern Hemisphere to those learnt in the Southern Hemisphere (see Note 2 in Chapter 5).

The same applies to the influence of the stars. The heavens we see above us are made from the light of stars that began travelling anything up to 12 billion years ago. Many of the stars we see may actually have ceased to exist millions of years ago, which is why I feel their influence is questionable. In terms of measurable effects on us, we know that the gravitational and electromagnetic influence of the stars we see is basically insignificant, thus I see no reason why the influence of their other energies should be any different. Modern science also indicates that more than 90 per cent of matter in the universe is unseen 'dark matter'. Why should light-emitting matter affect us more? Also, stars are basically hydrogen condensed from interstellar space. Why should the matter affect us more just because it has aggregated into one lump?

Can second-hand goods have 'bad Feng Shui'?

This concern is based on the fact that second-hand goods might have been around evil people, or part of an environment in which crimes, including acts of violence, took place, thus being 'tainted'. I wouldn't worry about this too much, as matter and energy are constantly being re-circulated.

Many years ago I read about the following calculation: each molecule of water we drink has, on average, been drunk before by eleven human beings, to say nothing of assorted animals and fish! I suspect a similar story exists for the various atoms and molecules we breathe and eat. The food you eat might have been grown in a field where a murder was committed, processed in a factory owned by an evil businessman, transported in a truck by a driver who was a terrorist, and sold to you by a shop assistant who was a member of the local Mafia! Furthermore, remember those water molecules. How many of those drinkers could have been murderers? Statistically, with the number of water molecules (which, remember, will all have been drunk by different people), every glass you drink will contain the molecules drunk by any number of people with a suspect history! That being the case, I don't think you need to be too fussed about a second-hand book!

And if you are going to worry about the bad Feng Shui associated with second-hand goods, why not worry about the bad Feng Shui that might be attached to new goods? The new wooden furniture you buy may come from trees grown in a forest where a murder was committed, and have been cut and assembled in a factory owned by criminals.

The point is that new goods could potentially have bad Feng Shui in the same way that second-hand ones could. I don't fuss too much about this because I assume there to be a far greater amount of good than evil in the world, and so each time I eat, drink, breathe or buy a new or second-hand item, I am probably bringing far more of the former into my environment than the latter. In the case of second-hand items of furniture, I assume that if the article were so tainted then the nature of its energy would make it unlikely that I would be tempted to buy it in the first place. Would I buy a second-hand item that I knew had been present in an environment in which a murder had been committed? Of course not; but more because of the negative associations this would raise in my mind each time I saw the object.

If second-hand goods having bad Feng Shui is still an area of concern to you, then perform regular cleansing or purification of your house if it makes you feel better. But don't worry too much if you get a gift of some antique jewellery!

If Feng Shui is so useful, how did the Mongols conquer the Chinese in their 'golden age' of Feng Shui?

A very good question, one that makes sure we keep Feng Shui in perspective! The energy of the environment is not the only factor in our lives. It is an important one, but no more important than such things as diet, exercise and proper rest.

No matter how good your Feng Shui is, drink to excess on a frequent basis and you will probably ruin your life. The same goes for such things as gambling. Ask any Feng Shui consultant to put their entire assets on a horse race and I can tell you the response you will get. If the Feng Shui experts can't manage to win at gambling, why should you!

The Chinese believe very much in personal virtue, effort, luck and destiny and it is often difficult to separate these things. Feng Shui can supplement them but not replace them. And thank goodness, too. Who would want to live in a world where those who had the money and power could simply corner the best Feng Shui spots and perpetuate their wealth and power forever. We only have to take a look at the typical ends to which the Chinese emperors came in order to see that even the most powerful and wealthy (with the best Feng Shui advice available) still needed virtue, effort and, yes, sometimes a little luck, to live well and die a peaceful death.

Is Feng Shui ethical?

If you regard chi as a limited resource (like land), then collaring more than your fair share does not seem very ethical. Consider, however, what the concept of being able to improve your environmental energy implies — that the energy condition of the environment can be made more beneficial for people as a whole. Feng Shui is too often seen in terms of striving for individual wealth and profit. Now, there is nothing wrong with these, but they should form part of a balanced life that involves productivity and creativity, as well as the amassing of wealth and the consumption of things. It is encouraging that many clients now seem to want to use Feng Shui as much to improve their personal relationships as to add to their wealth.

In short, there is no reason why we cannot be altruistic about Feng Shui — trying to improve the Feng Shui of our local environment for the benefit of all.

Chapter 2

Creating a Personal Energy Profile — Identifying Your Environmental Energy Needs

Your energy needs

It's a point often missed by those new to Feng Shui that it's *your* environmental energy needs that are important. We are not surprised when the exercise programs developed for young men or women are different for those over sixty, or that the dietary needs of a six-month-old baby are different from those of an adult, or that the required kilojoule intake of a mountaineer is different from that of an office worker. Should we be surprised, then, that the environmental energy needs of individuals also vary widely?

Most Feng Shui books are written from the point of view of a mythical 'average' person, with 'average' environmental energy needs. Alternatively, the focus of these books is often restricted to elements common to all Feng Shui practices, such as identifying and removing negative energy impacts. However, this is only a small part of Feng Shui, and focusing solely on this makes Feng Shui seem very negative; a bit like diets that talk only about what you should exclude, not what you should include. Neither focus is very likely to succeed in promoting the 'click' in our lives. If you want to achieve this click, you must:

1 identify those aspects of your life that need changing;

2 identify adjustments you can make in your environment that
will promote the changes you have identified.

To give you the tools to do this I will be outlining the following
concepts:
- chi;
- yin and yang;
- the eight major life energy areas;
- the eight environmental energies;
- the five elemental energy phases.

At this stage, the names will all sound very mysterious but, as you
will learn, they are simple, common sense ideas that are easy to learn
and apply. Also, these concepts are introduced in such a way that as
you progress, you won't be simply learning theory but will be
applying this knowledge to your life — identifying facts concerned
with the nature of your personal energy and how you may want to
change it.

At various points, you will be asked to enter information in a
personal energy profile (a personal energy profile table and form are
provided at the end of this chapter). This information will be
fundamental to the success of your whole positive Feng Shui
program, so you will need to treat updating this table with due care
and consideration.

By the end of Chapter 2, you will have identified where you want
to go in changing the nature of your energetic environment. Chapter
3 of the book will then deal with identifying the particular actions
that you can take to achieve these changes, and with building these
actions into a cohesive and systematic program — your own personal
positive Feng Shui program.

More about chi

Chi energy
We have described how the traditional Chinese saw the world around
them as an 'ocean' of energy called chi (sometimes written 'qi', 'ki'
or 'chee'). Not only Feng Shui, but all traditional Chinese arts and
practices, such as acupressure, Tai Chi, nutritional principles,

massage, meditation, calligraphy, etc., are based on the harmonisation and regulation of chi. When you understand chi, you have the key to many Chinese 'treasures'.

Chi is often translated as 'life energy', which is somewhat misleading as it can lead one to think that this energy only concerns living things. The term 'animating' energy is a much better translation, as the Chinese maintain that all the activity and change that occur within the universe is driven by chi. Another way of looking at things is seeing the whole universe as a living, evolving organism. Some bits of the universe might be more self-aware than others, but all is living. The Chinese often describe chi as 'the breath of the universe'.

If this sounds a bit mystical, it's actually far from it. Modern science actively pursues just such a unified concept. For example, science once viewed electricity and magnetism as two separate forces. Subsequent investigation showed that what was seen were just different aspects of one energy, now called 'electromagnetism'.

Modern scientists explain the entire known workings of the universe with four types of energy — electromagnetism, gravity, the strong nuclear force and the weak nuclear force. (When we perceive such things as heat and light, they are simply properties of these four major forces.) Just as electricity and magnetism have been unified into the concept of electromagnetism, science seeks to demonstrate that these four energies are themselves simply properties of one underlying energy. This elemental energy has not yet been given a name in the West but if we were to call it chi, we would be using the term in much the same way as the Chinese intended it to be used.

In other words, our day-to-day experiences of heat, light, sound, electricity, microwaves, etc., are simply partial glimpses of chi at work. Think of a child's picture card on which the image seems to change as it is moved past the eyes. In actual fact, the card remains exactly as it is but the change in viewing position alters our experience of what we see on the card. So it is with our experiences of chi.

This is not just academic theorising. If the energies that we see around us are all aspects of chi, then these same energies can tell us something about the underlying nature of the chi that generates them. Within any environment, an examination of its physical components (such as landforms and buildings) and its energies (such as light, sound, moisture, heat, aroma, movement and bio-energy) can tell us something about the quantity and quality of the underlying chi in that environment. From this, it is a small step to adjusting that chi.

For instance, the size, shape and appearance of landforms and physical structures (including buildings and furniture) can tell us about the chi energy 'frozen' within their structure. If we know these things tell us about the chi within an environment, we know that when we change these things we also change the chi within the environment, and thus change that environment's energetic effect on us. Feng Shui deals with 'diagnosing' and 'enhancing' environmental chi.

If you still worry that you don't understand chi and that you will therefore not be able to do Feng Shui, consider for a moment how good an explanation you could give in answer to questions such as 'What is electricity?', 'What is light?' and 'What are microwaves?' Despite the fact that we use these energies in our everyday lives, most of us would struggle to come up with a reasonable answer because, while we use them, we don't understand them. But does it matter? We plug in an appliance, turn it on and use it. All we really have to understand is how we can use electricity safely for our benefit. We can take a similar approach to chi. What we really need to know is: where can we find it and what can we do with it?

It may also help to visualise your environment as providing you with a chi diet. As in a food diet, we can get too much or too little chi. Just as we have major food groups and we need to get a reasonable balance of these in our diets, so we need different types of chi. Also, the quality of the chi is as important as the quality of our food; thus we should try to avoid tainted items. Finally, as discussed above, our food diet is an individual thing that depends on age, lifestyle and individual needs. Our requirements for chi are affected by the same sort of requirements, and whether we are talking about food or chi there is no one right diet for everyone.

We can deepen our understanding of chi by expanding the analogy of chi as an 'ocean of energy' to chi being more similar in nature to the entire water cycle.

The water cycle starts with the heat of the sun on the ocean, causing evaporation. The evaporated moisture may collect as clouds

SIMPLE WATER CYCLE

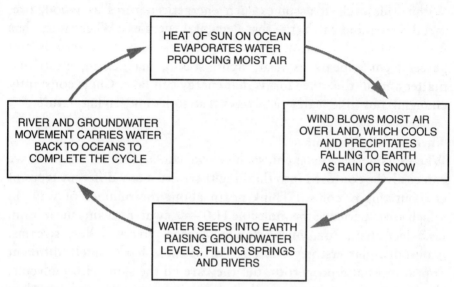

HEAT OF SUN ON OCEAN
EVAPORATES WATER
PRODUCING MOIST AIR

RIVER AND GROUNDWATER
MOVEMENT CARRIES WATER
BACK TO OCEANS TO
COMPLETE THE CYCLE

WIND BLOWS MOIST AIR
OVER LAND, WHICH COOLS
AND PRECIPITATES
FALLING TO EARTH
AS RAIN OR SNOW

WATER SEEPS INTO EARTH
RAISING GROUNDWATER
LEVELS, FILLING SPRINGS
AND RIVERS

and drift over the land. Depending on the temperature, it may fall to the earth as rain, snow, hail or sleet. Rain, melted snow and ice are either absorbed by the land, to emerge later as springs, or flow immediately into streams and rivers, where they return to the ocean from which they came.

This is, of course, a very simplified version of the water cycle, which actually includes other cycles within it. Groundwater captured by plants can be released into the air via the process of transpiration (to become clouds and fall once more as rain, or the plant is eaten by an animal, which sees the water within it go through yet another process). Round and round the water goes, sometimes returning quickly to the ocean, sometimes being caught for millennia in frozen ice, or deep within the earth.

Chi has its own cycle of change that is very similar to this, involving the change between the yin and yang conditions of chi. (Yin and yang are simple, but subtle, concepts, which are dealt with later in this chapter. For now, understand that the yang phase of the chi cycle is similar in nature to that part of the water cycle where the water is evaporated from the sea and moves over the land; the yin phase is similar to where the water vapour condenses, falls as rain onto the land and then runs down as rivers and streams to the sea.) Within this cycle it assumes such energetic natures as wood, fire, metal, water and earth (the five elemental energies). Where water has forms as varied as snow, ice, streams, fogs, clouds, waterfalls and geysers, chi appears as heat, light, sound, magnetism, electricity, matter and all the other forms that energy can take. Chi is constantly changing but (like water) is always true to its underlying nature.

There is only one chi!
When such terms as *sha* chi, *si* chi, *sheng* chi, and so on, are used, we can easily be confused into thinking there are many different types of chi, but this is not so. Think again about the number of ways in which we experience the molecule H_2O — as water, steam, snow, rain, ice, sleet, hail, fog, mist, clouds, oceans, rivers, lakes, streams, waterfalls, glaciers, geysers, etc. All of these have widely different appearances and properties, but they are all the same H_2O molecule. However, just as the terms 'ice', 'snow', 'rain', etc., are useful in telling us what to expect from the H_2O molecule in the form in which it currently appears, let's look at a few of the descriptions of chi to see what they tell us about it.

When using chi terminology, there are some Chinese terms that simply can't be translated into English (such as yin and yang), so the only solution is to use the Chinese word. However, this book takes the viewpoint that, to make understanding easier, where such terms can be translated into English they should be. (It seems that a lot of Chinese words get used in relation to chi, either to add a touch of mystery or to impress readers with the writer's ability.)

Si chi (deficient chi)
This is the description given to chi when there is not enough animating energy to support the environment around it. Think of the results of a prolonged dry spell on your garden, when the vegetation (and the life it supports) become weak and start to die off, with little new growth. In such cases, the remedy would be to water the garden using artificial sources. Feng Shui provides the same solution to problems of deficient chi by seeking to strengthen and increase the chi present in the natural environment.

When selecting an environment in which to live or work, it makes sense to avoid those generally deficient in chi, because it is always going to be an uphill battle to create a supportive environment. You can grow crops in a desert, but it's hard work — with a high risk of failure!

Sha chi (excess chi)
Sha chi is often translated as 'evil' chi, thus raising all sorts of fearsome images. This is more of a translation problem, as sha actually means 'excess'. It must be remembered that the name is applied on the basis of what the energy does, not what the energy is. If chi moves too fast or in too great a quantity it is called sha chi because of the damage it can do; *not* because the chi itself has become evil (any more than air becomes evil when it becomes part of a tornado or water becomes evil when it becomes part of a raging torrent).

There is nothing inherently good or bad about molecules of H_2O. The same molecules that almost drown us one day in a storm-tossed sea can save our life a year later as they bubble out of the ground in a desert oasis. Similarly, while small quantities of slowly flowing chi act to sustain life, large quantities of faster-flowing chi can injure our health. Thus, when Feng Shui writers speak of 'evil' chi and 'poison arrows' of chi (see below) understand that it is the same as describing typhoons as 'devil winds'. All this really means is that the same air molecules are moving around too fast for our liking. When the storm has passed, those air molecules will help keep us alive as we breathe them in.

Sha chi is often found associated with sharp corners, angles, and objects that point towards you. This is because chi is able to flow around curved surfaces, but on sharp corners, etc., flows directly ahead. This is generally what is referred to as a 'poison arrow'. Consider the same effect in nature; if you put a sharp-angle bend in a river you invite disaster!

So, references to 'evil' chi should not be taken literally. The Feng Shui solution is to slow and reduce it, so that the chi can reassume its beneficial qualities. Many talk of deflecting sha chi by the placement of mirrors and so forth. This is roughly analogous to discovering some garbage in your house or garden, and getting rid of the problem by tossing it into the street or over your neighbour's fence! It is better to clear up the problem properly, by dispersing or transforming the chi into more beneficial forms. The exact techniques for doing this are dealt with later in the book.

The real danger with sha chi is the modern focus on 'more is better'. Thus, in an effort to get more and more wealth, people seek to put more and more energy into aspects of the environment that support wealth, by, for example, building up the quantity and yang nature of energy in the wealth area of the house (the precise techniques for doing this are covered in Chapter 4). Eventually sha chi conditions are created—and all their good work is undone. This is why the positive Feng Shui program continually emphasises balance and harmony.

Stagnant chi

Stagnant chi is a Western name given to the aspect of Si Chi in which the flow of chi is too slow. Like water or air, chi can become stagnant and polluted if it does not move or flow. Again, let us use the image of water in your garden. This time you have a drainage problem. The water sits in the garden in stagnant pools; the plant roots rot; the balance of micro-organisms changes, replacing the life-giving aerobic bacteria with anaerobic bacteria; the air becomes foul with the metabolic wastes of these bacteria, such as methane. The solution lies not only in soaking up the excess water but by improving drainage, so that fresh water can flow in and through the garden. The Feng Shui approach to stagnant chi is similar. Get the chi moving again so it can reassume its beneficial qualities.

No matter what you are seeking to achieve with Feng Shui, your Feng Shui program should seek to identify and remove any environmental factors, such as clutter, that are indicative of stagnant chi.

Sheng chi

This is a term not easily translated. It means that the chi of the environment is balanced in respect of the individual, and provides healthy and beneficial surroundings. Sheng chi is the name we give to chi when the flow and quality is just right; it is the beneficial state of chi aimed at in the positive Feng Shui program. It is when we get an environment full of sheng chi that we should anticipate achieving the 'click' in our lives.

Quality of chi

Feng Shui writers often talk about the quality of chi, which simply means how good or bad the particular chi is for you. It is important to understand that here we are not talking about too little or too much chi, or chi that flows too quickly or too slowly, but the more subtle impact that a particular quality of chi may have upon us.

'Quality' of chi sometimes implies its 'purity'. However, you need to understand that the chi itself does not change, only its effect. Returning to the H_2O molecule, where a bucket of cold water being poured over you might be unpleasant, a bucketful of boiling water poured over you would be dangerous. All that has been done to change the 'quality' of the water is to change its temperature; the H_2O molecules are still the same, but their effects are different.

To use another analogy, a bell may emit a pure tone when struck. If the bell is cracked, the sound may be discordant. Either way, we are still just talking about sound waves; it is only the effect the sound waves have on us that has changed. We may, of course, tune a musical instrument to create pure tones, which we enjoy, and something similar can be done with chi. When we 'tune' chi to be more beneficial to us, we often talk about it becoming more pure or having a higher quality.

Chi vibrations and frequencies

Energy is vibration (or, in modern scientific parlance, 'waves'). Looking at the wave or vibratory nature of chi can often increase our understanding of it. Let's take a brief look at colour to see why this should be so.

Our perception of colour arises from changes in the frequency of light ('frequency' just means how many light waves we get in a certain space). It does not change the nature of 'what' is making the wave. Using a prism (or the water droplets in a rainbow), you can split 'white' light (light as it comes from the sun) into a spectrum of colours, from red to yellow to blue, and all the shades in between. Conversely, if you spin a multicoloured piece of cardboard fast enough, all the colours merge back into white light.

Even more amazingly, if you travel fast enough away from the source where the light is coming from, the colour will be 'red shifted' in comparison to how the light appears to someone moving more slowly away from the same light source. Thus, the same light (and, in fact, all frequencies of the electromagnetic spectrum) can appear different to different observers at the same time, depending on their relative speed. Since different colours have different psychological impacts, the same light, appearing as different colours to different observers, can have differing effects on those observers at the same time. It is, indeed, a fascinating universe in which we live!

When we talk about the electromagnetic spectrum, we are simply talking about the different numbers of waves of the same energy in the same space. This simple change in frequency (or vibration) allows us to experience effects that range from infra-red, to visible light, to ultraviolet, to radio waves, to X-rays, and so on. Some of these frequencies are healthy for our bodies, some are useful for our technologies, but it is all the same thing. Chi is like this: at some frequencies it is good for us; at others it has negative effects. When people talk about adjusting the quality of chi, think of it as adjusting the frequency of the energy.

Feng Shui and El Niño

Most people living around the edges of the Pacific Ocean are more than familiar with the El Niño effect. However, how many of us see this process as a pointer to the intricacies that can occur within simple energy flows? How many of us see it as a guide to how these energy flows can reach out to touch millions of lives in diverse ways?

The El Niño effect is the result of fluctuations in one of these energy flows, but it is far from fully understood. One belief is that the rise of sea temperatures in the eastern Pacific causes the eastern Pacific currents to slacken; another is that changes in sea levels (caused by winds and monsoons) cause the current to back up. Whatever the cause, the result is warmer water in the eastern Pacific. The resulting increase in evaporation there culminates in rainstorms, floods and blizzards over the west coasts of North and South America, while reduced evaporation in the western Pacific results in droughts in South-East Asia and Australia.

Weather reports now have daily information on the Southern Oscillation Index, which provides a guide as to the onset of the El Niño effect. A small shift in ocean temperature (or temporary rise in ocean levels) may have effects as severe as drought or flood for some places, or, for others, there will merely be a change in how much time people spend watering the garden.

As the El Niño effect comes and goes, prosperity shifts from area to area, with the financial and physical health of millions of individuals changing every time there are small movements in temperature or sea level. Of course, as prosperity levels change, relationships become more (or less) stressed, depending on the direction of movement; thus, achievement of the 'click' is moved closer or further away.

El Niño is but one aspect of 'weather' — simply the by-product of our planet's process of redistributing the energy received from the sun. This redistribution of energy tends to occur through thermal currents that establish themselves within the earth's ocean and atmosphere. Most of us are familiar with the larger, more permanent, of these energy flows (should we say 'dragon veins' (see below)), such as the Gulf Stream and the trade winds, and, in Australia, the more local energy flow known as the Fremantle doctor — the cooling, onshore breeze which Perth citizens welcome in the hot summer months.

This relationship of all aspects of our lives to changes in energy flow in the environment is a perfect example of the way in which Feng Shui works. You might say that there is nothing much an individual can do about the El Niño effect, but we can, to some degree, compensate for these effects on our energetic environment. For example, we might not be able to stop the drought that El Niño causes but we might be able to come up with various ways of maintaining moisture energy in our farm, garden or living environment, that will reduce the effects of drought; we might be able to protect against floods; choose land more wisely; or adapt our business strategy to changing prosperity levels.

Interestingly enough, while the Chinese people who developed Feng Shui knew nothing whatsoever about El Niño, application of the art provides a very satisfactory way of dealing with the effects that El Niño creates. This is because it puts us in touch with our environment and trains us to observe changes, at the same time providing us with the tools to compensate for them. There will always be some changes too vast to deal with (just as modern medicine has little to offer someone who falls into a volcano) and although Feng Shui cannot eliminate these, it can improve the odds of dealing with them successfully.

Dragon veins

This is another term that you will come across in Feng Shui books. Water flows through our planet in the form of rivers and streams, periodically accumulating in the form of lakes, oceans, clouds and underground aquifers. Chi flows and accumulates in much the same way. The rivers and streams of chi are sometimes referred to as the 'dragon veins'. (When chi flows within the human body, we talk about it flowing through channels and meridians, and accumulating in such areas as the *tan tien* or other energy centres.)

We know that electromagnetic energy flows in much the same way. If you want to see the dragon veins of a magnetic field, then place a magnet under a piece of paper and sprinkle iron filings on the surface of the paper. The dragon veins of chi are no more or less mysterious than the magnetic lines of force which weave their way through our world.

Now that we understand a little more about the nature of chi, it is time to turn to the next important concept: yin and yang. This allows us to describe our personal energy in a manner in which it becomes possible to understand whether changes to our environment will move us closer to, or further away from, achieving the 'click'.

Yin and yang

I doubt whether there are two Chinese words more familiar to the West than 'yin' and 'yang'. (Neils Bohr, the scientist who pioneered the modern atomic theory, incorporated the yin yang symbol in his family's coat of arms because he maintained it was the most perfect description of the workings of the universe.) However, I also doubt whether there are two words more misunderstood! Yin and yang are so central, not only to Feng Shui but to all the traditional arts and techniques developed by the Chinese, that it is worth spending a little time to ensure that you have a reasonable understanding of how to apply the concept.

The Chinese originally defined yang as the sunlit side of a mountain and yin as the shady side. This was a brilliant definition because while pointing out the differences between yin and yang, it also made it clear that neither side of the mountain was inherently yin or yang. Depending on the time of day (where the sun was), the morning yang side of the mountain became the afternoon yin side, and vice versa. The mountain sides were not yin or yang in themselves, they were yin or yang in comparison to each other, and which was yin and which was yang changed with the cycle of the day.

Also, if we compare a glass of cold water with a glass of boiling water, we say that the glass of cold water is yin in respect to the glass of boiling water. However, if we compare a glass of cold water with a glass of ice, that same glass of cold water is now yang in respect of the glass of ice. This point is worth labouring because errors are often made in classifying objects as yin or yang in themselves, resulting in mistakes being made by people trying to achieve energy changes in their environment. For example, you may see pine trees listed as yin (as they are in comparison to animal life) and so plant pine trees to make the energy more yin. However, if your garden previously consisted only of soft grasses and plants you could actually be making the energy of your garden more yang, as pine trees are yang in respect of grass and other soft, low-growing plants.

One of the reasons for labelling two things as yin or yang is that we then know which way the chi will flow between two objects. It will always flow to bring about balance and harmony between yin and yang. If you encounter something cold, then it will make you colder and itself warmer. The chi will flow to make the yang less yang and the yin less yin.

In many ways, this is simply a statement of the second law of thermodynamics, which says that if you have two areas containing different levels of energy, the energy levels will tend to equalise. However, whereas the second law of thermodynamics is depressing (it predicts the eventual heat death of the universe), the theory of yin and yang is much more positive, because it includes the premise that yin and yang generate each other.

Thus, the Taoists refer to the time before the physical universe as *wu* chi — the 'pregnant void'. As this description suggests, rather than a sterile nothingness, wu chi represents the potential for everything that can possibly be. (See the Chinese creation diagram on page 45. This explanation of the beginning of the universe, taken from the 'Tao Teh Ching' by the Taoist philosopher Lao Tse, is over

2500 years old but is remarkably consistent with modern cosmological theories.) Our universe represents only part of this potential — that based on the current physical laws (other physical laws may exist for other universes). When our universe runs down, or ceases to exist, another potential *must* realise itself. That is because when such a condition occurs it represents extreme yin, which then, by its very nature, generates yang (the next universe); a much happier thought!

If you ask me why yin must always generate yang, I will answer you when you tell me why any physical law should be so! In the case of physical laws, all modern science can do at its present level of knowledge is describe them, not explain them. Physical laws are determined from observation of what we see happen, and so is the concept of yin and yang.

The Chinese believe that the small reflects the large. We see daily evidence that the cycle of life and death is always contained within larger cycles. The individual lives and dies but the species goes on; the species dies but the biosphere goes on; the biosphere dies, but presumably new biospheres are created on new planets.

The theory of yin and yang can be comfortably accommodated within any religion or belief system. It is simply a tool.

Yin and yang on a more earthly level
Another (less cosmic) way to think of the concept of yin and yang is to equate it with the positive and negative poles of a battery. When a wire is connected from the negative to the positive pole (bringing yin and yang into contact), a current of electrons starts to flow. This current can be transformed into many other energies, such as light, heat, radio waves and mechanical motion.

In a like manner, when wu chi became Tai Chi (when the potential for the universe became actual), yin and yang were simultaneously created. Instantly, chi began to flow and this flow created the '10,000 things' (all things that exist). This is the meaning of the Chinese diagram shown opposite.

It is important to note that it is the direction of flow that makes the difference between the positive and negative current. Identical electrons are flowing round the circuit; however, in the positive wire they flow towards the place where they will do work and in the

CHINESE DIAGRAM OF CREATION

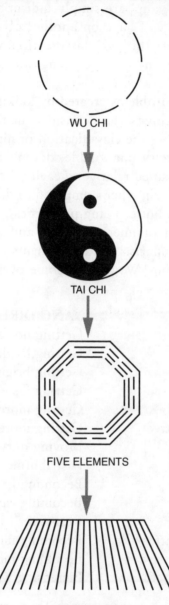

WU CHI

TAI CHI

FIVE ELEMENTS

'10,000' THINGS

negative wire they flow back to the source of power. Take away either wire and no current flows. Chi can only be generated when there is differentiation of yin and yang.

Is it yin or is it yang?

The terms 'yin' and 'yang' are simply indications of the effect that one object or energy will have on another object or energy. People who yearn for certainty through classification, wanting to have a list of what are yin things and what are yang things, are thus doomed to disappointment.

To understand the problems created by looking at yin and yang as innate properties of 'things', let's consider the most common item to appear on such a list — the classification of night as yin and day as yang. This sounds pretty unarguable, doesn't it? However, yin and yang can only be classified relative to each other. Thus, day on earth would be classified as yin when compared to day on Mercury, where it's a lot brighter and hotter (yang properties); a winter's day would be yin compared to a summer's day. Yin and yang are not 'things', they are terms of comparison and statements about the direction in which energy is moving. We can list some of these directions, as in the table below.

YIN DIRECTION	YANG DIRECTION
Getting colder	Getting hotter
Getting quieter	Getting louder
Getting darker	Getting brighter
Getting slower	Getting faster
Getting denser	Getting more dispersed
Getting more intuitive	Getting more analytic/scientific
Moving inward	Moving outward
Gathering	Distributing
Becoming softer	Becoming harder
Becoming flaccid	Becoming rigid
Yielding	Resisting
Becoming more matter-like	Becoming more energy-like
Becoming more passive	Becoming more active
Shortening wavelength	Increasing wavelength*

*This classification may seem counter-intuitive. The change in wavelength occurs as frequency increases or decreases. We would expect an increase in frequency to be a yang attribute; however, as frequency increases, the waves themselves become shorter and denser (more waves in a given space), which is a yin attribute. Thus, long wavelength (low frequency/red) is yang and short wavelength (high frequency/blue) is yin in effect. Nature goes on to prove the point by showing that if the wave density is increased enough, we start getting things which behave more like matter — yin.

Confusion sometimes sets in because white-hot things are hotter than red-hot things. So, a blue–white star is actually yang in comparison to a red star. But how does this reconcile with the fact that the colour red, as compared to blue, is yang in terms of its effect on living things? It is because we have confused material things (in this case, stars and other hot objects) with the energies they give out (in this case the colour aspect of those energies).

More thoughts on yin and yang

You will notice from the table that there are no 'good' or 'bad' aspects of yin or yang. Good and evil are not yin and yang complements, and nor are concepts such as weak and strong, or right and wrong. You must be careful when thinking of yin as negative and yang as positive, that judgments are not implied, any more than you would make judgments when talking about negative and positive electric currents.

The terms 'female' and 'male' are often used as yin/yang complements but this can also be misleading. In our culture, the female is often seen as more intuitive, more yielding, more emotional than the male, who is seen as more scientific, more resistant and less emotional. These are generalisations, not facts. Take any male and female and measure them in accordance with the above attributes. The female may well be more yang than the male and the male more yin than the female. A young person is yang in respect to an old person, so how do we categorise a young female as compared to an older male? If body is yin and mind yang, how do we categorise a female scientist in comparison to a male dancer? Dancing is not feminine per se, and you're welcome to argue the case with a Russian Cossack dancer or a Maori warrior performing a Hakka!

Furthermore, even if one accepted the cultural generalisations, it would not be natural that because female is yin in respect to male that a female should only have yin characteristics. This is about as logical as noting that since the lower half and back of the body is yin, while the upper half and front are yang, it is not natural for females to have top halves and fronts!

You will also see such things as a spoon and a knife categorised as yin and yang. This, again, confuses function with object. The act of containing and gathering is yin, the act of cutting or separating yang, but does that make spoons yang and knives yin? Only if all you are looking at is the containing and cutting aspect. For instance, is an old, lightweight, dull-edged, white plastic knife yin or yang in respect of a new, heavy, sharp-edged red metal spoon? What happens if you eat peas off your knife and use your spoon to cut up a slice of cake? Assumptions that you can categorise objects as yin/yang in themselves, rather than by their specific effect on other specific objects, will always lead to confusion and contradiction.

Yin, yang and you

It should now be clearly understood that the terms 'yin' and 'yang' are simply ways of looking at energy relationships. Using this concept, you can now adapt your table of yin and yang directions to apply to yourself and see in which direction you wish to move. If you wish to move mainly in a yang direction, then see yourself as yin in comparison to where you want to be. If you wish to move mainly in a yin direction, then see yourself as yang in comparison to where you want to be. You can look at the direction in which you want to move as your 'energy objective'.

You may feel a little or a lot out of balance. If your life has 'clicked', then you may feel you are just about where you should be; thus you should carefully assess any changes you might make that could shift this balance.

The first step in assessing the condition of personal energy is to determine its overall yin–yang balance. You can gain a good idea of the nature of this balance by looking at the type of improvements you are seeking in life. For instance, consider the following examples.

Case 1 — yin imbalance

If your energy is too yin, then the benefits you would expect from making your energy more yang are:

• getting more done in life (you will find that you have the energy to start more projects and not run out of steam before completing them; you will do more with your family and others with whom you have relationships; you will also be able to put more into your career and personal development);

- becoming more assertive;
- your willpower increasing;
- feeling more energised, happier; generally less subject to depression;
- life seeming richer in experience.

Case 2 — yang imbalance

If your energy is too yang, then the benefits you would expect from making your energy more yin are:

- again, getting more done in life! (you will find that you have the focus and concentration to see projects through, rather than being distracted by new projects before completing the first ones);
- your relationships with your family and friends tending to be deeper and more relaxed, with less tendency to disagreement;
- reduction in conflict and increase in focus allowing you to achieve more in your career and personal development;
- feeling more centred, relaxed and balanced, less likely to be thrown by outside events, and less subject to neurotic behaviour;
- life seeming richer in experience.

What now?

Decide, overall, if your objective is to become more yang and less yin (as in Case 1) or more yin and less yang (as in Case 2). This becomes your personal energy objective.

Now complete 'Direction' in the Personal Energy (Evaluation) Profile form in column 2 (this is Form 1 on page 59).

Determining your personal energy approach

It is important to remember that we are talking about balancing yin and yang. This balance can be achieved by taking either of two approaches — by increasing the energy that is deficient or decreasing the energy that is excessive. An example may make this clearer.

We can look at the yin–yang energy balance as we would a household budget, with yin being the income and yang being the expenditure. If we are spending more than we are earning, to balance the budget we can either increase income or decrease expenditure. On the other hand, if we are earning more than we spend, then we are in the happy circumstance of either being able to increase our spending or decrease our income.

Should your personal energy balance be achieved by increasing or decreasing total personal energy? This is, in itself, a question of balance. The general recommendation is that if there is more going on in your life than you wish to cope with, go for decreasing the total energy (decreasing yang). If your life is less rich in experience and activity than you would wish, go for increasing the total energy (increasing yin).

The *amount* of total personal energy is not the key factor but the *balance* of the energy is. Let's again use the analogy of the household budget. Provided the budget is balanced, does a bigger budget mean a happier and more fulfilled life? The answer is, of course, that some people live very happy and fulfilled lives on a very small budget, while others have an enormous budget and drag themselves through a life of misery and lack of fulfilment. Which approach you take will depend on your personal circumstances.

What now?
Decide which of the four basic energy approaches (increase yin, increase yang, decrease yin, decrease yang) is appropriate to the energy objective you identified on your personal energy profile, and record the selected approach number next to 'Approach' in the right-hand column of Form 1.

Table 1 is provided as a reference guide. These approach numbers will be used to guide you to the appropriate energy enhancement and balancing techniques used in the program.

Increasing the depth of your personal energy evaluation — the eight major life energy centres

Some of you will have found it very easy to categorise yourself as needing either Case 1– or Case 2–type improvements. Others will have found this more difficult, and some will be in a complete quandary. The reason for this is that the Chinese have determined that, just as our bodies are made up of different organ systems and each system can have its own degree of health relative to the rest of the body, one's life can also be broken down into major energetic activities. Each of these energetic activities can also have its own individual degree of 'health', or yin–yang balance.

This might sound complex but fortunately the Chinese have done the hard work for us and identified eight areas of major life energy centres. The selection of these areas is not arbitrary; it relates to the *ba gua*, which we will discuss in more detail later. For now, let's just list the areas (order does not reflect importance):

1 Career (purpose);
2 Wisdom (inner knowledge);
3 Health (family);
4 Wealth (prosperity);
5 Reputation (fame);
6 Relationships (with all creatures);
7 Creativity (children);
8 Helpful people (travel).

If you found it difficult to categorise yourself energetically on an overall basis (as Case 1 or Case 2) you would either have had:

• some of these eight major energetic activities with a yin balance, some with a yang balance, and maybe some already balanced; or

• you would be relatively balanced overall (if this is the case, you should be enjoying life!).

Conversely, if you found it easy to categorise yourself, you may have done so not because all the eight major life energy centres were all yin or yang but because your life is being dominated by one of those energy systems. For instance, if your life tends to be dominated by, say, career or relationships, then you may mistake the experiences you have in this one area of life as representing the energy balance of all the other areas of life. If you decide this is the case, there are things that can be done to rebalance your life (which we will be discussing later).

For reasons which will soon become apparent, when we look at what we want to do to get the 'click', we need to be sure that we have looked at all the eight life energy centres and that they are all balanced within themselves and against each other. To do this, we will need to know a little more about them.

Career (purpose)

An energetic activity, perhaps wider in scope than you might first think. Career should be understood as what we 'do' in life. This can mean your job, business, profession or vocation, but it does not have to be paid work. It is even possible that the work for which you are paid is not your real work in life but simply a way of financing that work. Career certainly includes such activities as homemaker and carer. Your career is most likely to be found in the answer you would give to the first question that was always directed to the guest in *Asimov's Black Widowers' Club*: 'How do you justify your existence?'

A child may not have a career but is certainly seeking (even if only subconsciously) a path, whereby they can contribute to society and justify their own existence. It is from such justification that feelings of self-esteem arise. When the energy in this area is in balance, a child will quickly and confidently be drawn to activities that will support any future career.

If retirement is regarded as the time when we cease to justify our own existence, thinking that we can live on the 'credit' of our past effort, our energy will become seriously unbalanced and it will be most unlikely that we will experience the 'click'. Readers will find their own justification for existence in this period, but the attempt to pass on one's own life wisdom to family and friends (even if it is only to identify the mistakes one has made) is an incredibly valuable contribution, that can be life-changing for others.

Do not confuse career with wealth and prosperity; your purpose in life is not the acquisition of wealth. Good remuneration and career may go together but just as often they do not.

Personal growth (education)

This area covers your knowledge, character, ethics and inner wisdom. These develop and change throughout your life — not always positively. Curiously, the major focus I see in this area is that of people trying to improve the education prospects of their children. Few seem worried about the ethics or inner wisdom of their children until a problem such as drugs, promiscuity, or participation in crime is struck, which then drives home their importance.

A famous scientist called A.H. Maslow identified a 'hierarchy' of needs, held by all human beings. The first need is food and shelter. Once this is achieved, relationships with others are sought. When this need is satisfied, we then seek what Maslow called 'self-actualisation'. This can best be described as personal growth, a need to develop and grow, to be the best we can be. If you want your life to 'click', you must feel that you are at least on that road of personal growth. Life is not simply about acquiring more qualifications and more facts, winning scholastic awards and getting into the best university (these areas are often simply seen as roads to wealth); it is about feeling that you are improving the person you are.

Health (family)

Health is too often seen as just happening, whereas it should be a real focus in our lives. What we drink, eat and breathe; where we live; how we exercise; how we structure our lives — all these things play a critical role in our health.

The Chinese often referred to this area as 'family' and it's easy to see how our family life impinges so strongly on all of the factors mentioned above. We all know how difficult it is to pursue a healthy life without the support of family. Also, it could almost be said that if we take care of what the family eats, drinks and breathes, where it lives, how it exercises and how its activities are structured, the health of the individual family member will take care of itself.

Furthermore, perhaps the connection of family and health reflects a responsibility to maintain health, not only for one's own benefit but for the good of the family. It's an approach to health that at least dilutes some of the 'me, me, me' focus that has crept into today's outlook on health.

Prosperity (wealth)

Prosperity is sometimes referred to as wealth, though I am far from sure that the two are the same. Wealth is often misunderstood, in the sense that people tend to feel they can always do with a little more, 'so let's increase the energy in this area as much as possible'. Not a good idea! An excess of yang energy in the wealth area can increase the volatility of wealth and the contention over wealth, rather than the degree of wealth!

There is nothing wrong with seeking enough wealth to live your desired life. You are unlikely to get the 'click' if you don't know where your next meal is coming from and the drawer is full of unpaid bills. Too often, however, the pursuit of wealth becomes the end, rather than a means to an end, and actually prevents achievement of the 'click'. It is particularly important to balance the energy and focus put into this aspect of life with the energy and focus put into the other areas.

Reputation (fame)

A reputation was once regarded as a person's most valuable possession. In today's society, reputation seems to have been de-emphasised. However, all energetic activities are interrelated and either mutually supportive or destructive, and a good reputation is important to career and relationships. I don't know many people who would say their lives have 'clicked' if their family, friends and associates all have low opinions of them.

'Reputation' is sometimes confused with 'fame', but being famous often just seems to mean being widely known, and not necessarily for anything important. Such fame seems to evaporate as quickly as it appears.

Ultimately, fame is only important in some careers, whereas reputation is important for *all* careers.

Relationships (with all creatures)

Maslow rated people's need for relationships as a little above the need for food and shelter. Without relationships, life is a pretty empty affair. Solitary confinement is still one of the worst punishments there is, and even to be ostracised by one's neighbours or workmates is not a happy experience for most. Give young monkeys everything they need to live except companionship, and they die. With humans, the ability (or opportunity) for a child to bond with others is critical, not only to the healthy development of the child's personality but to the child's health generally.

Relationships are not just about the bonds between partners and family members but can extend to any association where there is an emotional element, where you care for another person. I would even include the bonds that can be formed with pets. Certainly, studies have shown that people with such bonds tend to live five years longer on average than those who don't, so loving relationships between humans must clearly be very important!

Creativity (children)
Children are, perhaps, the ultimate act of creation; this is both in terms of procreation and in terms of bringing them up. The connection between creativity and children is attested to by the frequency with which we refer to organisations or projects that we have created as our 'children'. Creativity, of course, includes creativity in the arts, in business or even in such things as gardening.

All of us have creative ability. Again, however, do not assume that more energy in this area is always better. If you find yourself so creative you are always rushing off to start something new before finishing your other creations, this indicates too much unbalanced energy.

Support structures (helpful people, travel)
Support structures can simply be called 'helpful people'. The fact is, we create energy around us, which disposes people either to help or ignore us. Having mentors or patrons in life can make a world of difference to achieving the 'click'. When energy is strong in this area, we are credited with an ability to network.

You may be surprised to see travel included in this area. However, just as our lives can be supported by different people they can also be supported by exposure to different geographical and cultural environments. It has long been said that travel broadens the mind (which really means increases inner wisdom). The energy in this area will bring us into contact with people, organisations, cultures and places for which we have a need.

What now?
For each of the eight major life energy centres decide your:
• personal energy direction; and
• energetic approach.

Record the results in Form 1.

If you previously had difficulty in classifying your overall condition, you can now do the following:
- Where the majority of the eight life activities show a Case 1 situation, record a yin imbalance in row 1 of Form 1.
- Where the majority of the eight life activities show a Case 2 situation, record a yang imbalance in row 1 of Form 1.

You now have a personal energy profile that will allow you to determine what changes you want to make in each of your major life energy centres. The next step is to look at the energy of the environment itself, in order to learn how to create the most beneficial energy possible.

Some additional points

Monitoring changes in your personal energy

Your personal energy will change over time (there would be very little point in doing Feng Shui if it didn't), which means you should redo your personal energy profile at least every three months. This will allow you to detect changes that are occurring as a result of your Feng Shui program and provide confirmation as to its effectiveness.

Remember, Feng Shui is rarely instantaneous but it does develop its own momentum. If, for instance, you had moved into new premises at home or work a few weeks before doing your personal energy evaluation, you would not expect your personal energy to reflect fully the energetic changes that such a move would cause. These would only emerge over the upcoming months and years. (In the same way, if you gave up smoking you would not expect the full physical changes from stopping to occur the next day.) You might get some immediate changes but the important ones will take some time to emerge. Be realistic in your expectations of the speed of change.

Feng Shui of family members and other occupants of your dwelling, or of your business place

Too many people worry only about their own Feng Shui and disregard the interests of family members, whose Feng Shui requirements may be quite different to their own. Ideally all occupants of a dwelling should be encouraged to establish their own energy objectives. If some occupants are either not interested or too young to do this, there is nothing to stop you making such an evaluation on their behalf. It may not be fully accurate, but it will at least provide you with some guide. Where energy objectives of different occupants appear to conflict, the approach is to identify personal areas of the occupants, such as their bedroom, desk, favourite chair, etc., and carry out the Feng Shui work to improve these people's energy in these areas. This is dealt with further in Chapter 5.

It may not be practicable to involve all other occupants in the Feng Shui program, either because of age or lack of interest. However, should one or more of the other occupants appear to be having problems, either in getting their personal 'click' or in ways which are preventing you from getting yours. You can make copies of Form 1 and complete them on behalf of the other occupants, though it is better if they can complete them themselves. Try to reflect what you would expect the person's true self-assessment to be — not *your* judgment of them or what you think they would say about themselves rather than actually believe.

In order that privacy can be maintained, if required, the personal assessments are on different charts. Exactly how you resolve conflicting Feng Shui interests (if these should arise) is dealt with in Chapter 5.

Personal numbers and stars

Some readers may be surprised not to find any references to numerological and astrological aspects, that is, personal numbers and stars in conjunction with associated elements of the five elemental energies. You may have read about these in books based on the Flying Star school of Feng Shui techniques and other similar systems. Despite their mathematical appearance, these systems often involve intuitive assessments by Feng Shui masters and the systems carry significant risk of error when used on a self-assessment basis. If this is your area of interest, then you are advised to seek appropriate guidance from professional Feng Shui consultants, or be patient and start with personal energy evaluation and see the results that can be obtained from this approach. If desired, these techniques can be supplemented with personal numbers, stars and elements at a later stage.

Table 1 — Identifying personal energy objectives and approach

PERSONAL ENERGY OBJECTIVE	PERSONAL ENERGY APPROACH
Case 1 Excessive yin, deficient yang	Approach 1 — increase yang Approach 2 — decrease yin
Case 2 Excessive yang, deficient yin	Approach 3 — decrease yang Approach 4 — increase yin

Form 1 — Personal energy (evaluation) profile

QUESTION	YIN/YANG ASSESSMENT
1 In which direction do you wish your OVERALL energy balance to move?	DIRECTION ~~yang~~ *yang* ↑ *yang* *yin* APPROACH
2 In which direction do you wish your CAREER energy balance to move?	DIRECTION ~~yang~~ *yin* APPROACH ~~yang~~ ↗ *yang yin* ↓yang
3 In which direction do you wish your PERSONAL GROWTH energy balance to move?	DIRECTION ~~yang~~ APPROACH ↑ *yang*
4 In which direction do you wish your FAMILY energy balance to move?	DIRECTION ~~yang~~ *yin* APPROACH ~~yang~~ ↑ *yin*
5 In which direction do you wish your WEALTH AND ABUNDANCE energy balance to move?	DIRECTION ~~yang~~ *yin* APPROACH ↑ *yin*
6 In which direction do you wish your FAME AND REPUTATION energy balance to move?	DIRECTION ~~yang~~ APPROACH ↑ *yang*
7 In which direction do you wish your RELATIONSHIP energy balance to move?	DIRECTION ~~yang~~ *yin* APPROACH ↑yang ↓yang
8 In which direction do you wish your CREATIVE energy balance to move?	DIRECTION ~~yang~~ *yin* ↑ APPROACH *yin*
9 In which direction do you wish your SUPPORT energy balance to move?	DIRECTION ~~yang~~ APPROACH ↑yang

Chapter 3

Creating an Environmental Energy Profile — Building a Picture of Your Environment

Collecting information about your energy environment

This chapter deals with creating an energy profile of your environment. This environmental energy profile can then be matched against your personal energy profile, to see where the energy of your environment supports you in your aim of achieving the 'click' and where it works against you. Chapter 4 will then complete the process, by showing you how to adjust your environment to make it as supportive as possible.

As in Chapter 2, you will not only be learning how to use a number of Feng Shui concepts but will be gathering information essential to the later development of your positive Feng Shui program. This information will be entered on Form 2 located at the end of this chapter.

Remember, no environment will be wholly perfect from an energy perspective. Rather than becoming concerned about any negative aspects you might identify, focus more on the fact that through this Feng Shui program you will be improving the overall energetic effects of your environment.

Identifying your energetic environment

Before going any further, we need to be sure the term 'environment' is understood from a Feng Shui perspective. If you break down your overall energetic environment into smaller units, your Feng Shui program is easier to manage and target. We will start off by looking at the typical environments where we might expect to spend most of our time:

- home; ✓
- work; ✓
- study; ✓
- exercise; ✓
- religious or spiritual;
- holiday. ✗

If, apart from your home, you do not spend any significant amounts of time in any of the above environments, they can be ignored as far as your Feng Shui is concerned. As a general guideline, if less than an average of around fifteen hours per week, over several months, is spent in a particular environment, it is unlikely to have any significant impact.

Remember, an environment is a 'place'. If you spend twenty-five hours a week on sporting activities but at different locations, then each of these is a separate environment. Again, you would need to be regularly spending more than fifteen hours a week in each environment before it would be worth worrying about from a Feng Shui perspective. The same would be true if your work involved attending different locations.

If, as a number of retired Australians tend to do, the summer months are spent in the southern states and the winter months in the northern states, you would then have more than one home location and you would need to consider developing a Feng Shui program for each. Holiday environments are only likely to have impact if you have a holiday home and visit the one location regularly.

What now?
Turn to the positive Feng Shui program Form 2 on page 94, fill in the average number of hours spent in each environment and complete the attached questions. Remember, where you spend your time can vary,

so check for any significant changes every six months or so. If a significant change occurs, adjust the form accordingly.

Tips on selecting the environments to carry out your personal program

Use the home environment as your starting point
It would normally be expected that you would start off by looking at the home environment. The initial Feng Shui benefits are likely to be greater here because it has such an influence on your personal energy. It is this environment, also, over which you are likely to have the greatest control. Exceptions might be if you travel a lot, frequently changing living places but having a central and consistent workplace, or if you live where you work.

Don't try too much at one time!
It is recommended you make only a limited number of changes at any one time. Like exercise, Feng Shui is a lifetime activity. If you tried to cram a lifetime of exercise into one month you would not expect the results to be positive. Likewise, too many Feng Shui changes at one time stir up so much energy you would end up with an excess yang condition, no matter how beneficial the individual changes would be if taken one by one. Carrying out a limited number of changes also makes it much easier to see what the effects are of each Feng Shui action taken. If lots of changes are made at the one time, you will not know what is working and what is not.

Environmental components

Each of the environments listed may have a number of 'components':
• local area;
• land;
• building;
• rooms and major fixtures;
• furnishings and decorations.

Developing your Feng Shui program component by component makes it easier to manage, as not everything has to be dealt with at once. Again, the idea is to focus your efforts in the areas that have the most potential for improvement, bearing in mind the resources available to you. One of the greatest benefits of this procedure is that it allows you both to focus your efforts where you will get the best results and, over time, ensure you cover all the important areas of your environment.

To aid in the choice of component(s) on which you would like to focus, a brief outline of each has been provided. At this stage you need only understand enough about each component to select which of the modules (provided in Chapter 4) you are going to use in your program.

This section also includes information on the eight energy conditions, which will enable you to identify the influence the environmental component is having and how the energy conditions it creates can be enhanced to suit your needs.

Summary of the program development process

Step 1 — Identify your personal energy needs and objectives
Complete Form 1 of the Feng Shui development program, at the end of Chapter 2.

Step 2 — Identify your significant energetic environments
Complete Form 2 of the Feng Shui development program, at the end of this chapter.

Step 3 — Identify the program modules you will be using to create your personal Feng Shui program
This is the step on which we are currently working. There is one program module for each environmental component. Using Form 3 (at the end of Chapter 4), indicate the environmental component(s) you wish to include.

Step 4 — Complete your personalised Feng Shui program
This is done by working through the positive Feng Shui program modules selected in Step 3 above.

Step 5 — Keep your Feng Shui program current
Every six months, or sooner if you have a major lifestyle change such as a new house, a new job or a major new relationship, review Steps 1, 2 and 3, and amend the forms as appropriate.

Local area component

Once you have chosen a particular environment or place on which to work, you will need to decide how far the environment that influences you extends. The closer things are to you, the greater their relative effect. This means that the Feng Shui impact drops off quickly with distance and you soon come to a point where impact is negligible and can be disregarded. However, you should include the following:

- What you could see from your premises, in any direction, if they and any adjoining buildings were constructed completely of glass, including floors, walls, ceilings and boundary walls (if any). (Naturally, you would not be able to see under the ground but there are a number of influences here that we shall look at specifically.)
- What is carried to your property, on or through the air. Consider sound, light, aroma, moisture and the condition/movement of the air itself; the air may be fresh or polluted, or be high in either negative or positive ions. Prevailing wind patterns and what they pass over on the way to your dwelling is also important.

This will give a reasonably accurate picture of what constitutes your local environment.

Another good way of determining your local environment is to get hold of a street map showing the area around your premises for about a 1- or 2-kilometre radius. The direction of major geological features, such as mountain ranges, oceans, lakes, etc., that do not appear on the map should be noted, as should the direction of prevailing winds.

To aid in collecting relevant information about your local area, here is a list of important 'elements' you might consider:

- climate;
- geographical features (landforms);
- soil types;
- vegetation;
- buildings;
- roads;

- other transport facilities and activities;
- power plants and facilities.

Detailed information on these elements is provided in Chapter 4.

General considerations

All environments will have a local area component that has to be taken into account, whether it is the home or work, or any of the other, environments. There is generally not too much we can do to change the energetic nature of the local area. The value in looking at this component is in:

- determining whether or not you wish to purchase a home, establish a business, send your child to school, etc., in a particular local area; and
- identifying energetic conditions that are not supportive to you, your family members, your business or other activities, so that you can create the appropriate enhancements.

In terms of assessing the general level and condition of chi in the local area, we would also look at what we might call the 'abundance' or 'prosperity' factor of the area. This can be evidence of the existence of beneficial chi or a deficiency, excess or stagnation of chi.

Starting a business in a rundown, poor area is obviously going to be harder and more risky, thus you would have to be sure the business suited the area. If you already have a problem with excessive yang energy, buying a house in a busy city, rather than in a quiet suburban or rural area, could create problems. You should look at whether the area is predominantly urban, rural, suburban, business, retail, etc., and whether this suits the energy condition and activities that you, or you and your family, intend to undertake there.

Should you find your environment is not perfect, you don't have to up and move. Introduce the Feng Shui enhancements (discussed in Chapter 4) appropriate to your energy condition and you may successfully shift your Feng Shui energy balance.

You can use the eight environmental energy conditions to assess the nature and quality of the underlying chi. We are, of course, particularly interested in establishing the presence of sheng chi (beneficial chi) and the absence of such conditions as si chi (deficient chi), sha chi (excessive chi) and stagnant chi.

Land component

The land component deals with the land that 'belongs' to the house, business premises, school, or other building being evaluated. Obviously, Feng Shui does not recognise legal niceties relating to land ownership, so what is meant by 'belonging'?

In the case of your house, this is reasonably obvious — it is the block of land that you bought, that is surrounded by various visible boundaries. Where it merges into park land, bush land, etc., your land becomes that area surrounding your house that you see yourself as responsible for maintaining (whether or not you do so!). It does not matter (in respect of Feng Shui impact) whether you are in legal possession of the land or not; we might say it is our mental, emotional and perhaps even spiritual relationship with the land that is important. The stronger this is, the stronger the Feng Shui impact will be.

When you live in a block of units, the energetic effect of the land that belongs to that block of units is much reduced. There will, however, still be an effect. The same situation arises for separate businesses located in the same large buildings or complex. The degree of energetic impact will increase in proportion to the degree to which you see yourself as responsible for maintaining any part of that area. In that case, those parts you maintain should be viewed as 'your land'.

Land also has a number of elements, including:
- the actual make-up of the land itself — soil, rock types and mix, including artificial structures such as paths, driveways, courtyards and anything that covers the land;
- the shape of the land area;
- any slopes or changes in height of the land;
- water elements present on the land — ponds, streams, waterfalls (natural or artificial), moisture content of soil, underground streams and water pipes; natural humidity over land;
- the aspect of the land — the degree to which it receives sun and reflected light; also exposure to other elements, such as wind;
- electromagnetic elements — overhead or underground power

transmission lines, telephone lines, microwave transmission pathways, generators (as in pumps), elements distorting the natural geomagnetic field (many metal pipes may form natural electrical transmission lines);

- sound energy — for example, natural sounds from bush land or oceans and rivers; from roads and highways, or city background noise;
- aroma — as might be generated from flowers or other vegetation; rotting material; natural out-gassing, leaking gas pipes or storage tanks and cavities (water features generally have an aroma of some type);
- bio-energetic effects from vegetation and animal life; and
- moving energy aspects — as might result from animal and bird life, water features, wind movement through trees, movement of people and vehicles, artificial aspects such as fountains, windmills, etc.

General considerations

The land component of an environment may impact significantly on the energetic balance of an individual or business in a controllable way. Gardens surrounding houses, for instance, can have particular impact. Where land is communally owned (as with home units and many small businesses), the main purpose in looking at the land component is to identify energetic impacts you might want to enhance.

If your building covers all (or virtually all) of the land, then, for practical purposes, the land component of the environment can be ignored as far as the positive Feng Shui program is concerned, due to the fact that there are no opportunities to make Feng Shui changes to the land. In this instance, the eight environmental energy conditions are treated as elements of the building itself. As well as looking at the eight energy conditions you would examine the five elemental energy phases and water dragon aspect of the land, together with the *ba gua* relationships that exist. (Do not be too concerned about these aspects at this stage as they are examined in detail in Chapter 4.)

Building component

The first consideration here is whether all of the building 'belongs' to the person or business (the word 'belongs' being used in the same way as when relating to land). Where only part of a building belongs, that part that will have the greatest Feng Shui impact.

If you own a flat, focus your attention on this area rather than on the block as a whole. If you live in a house that is shared with others, then 'your building' is the part that belongs to you; a business would mainly be interested in that part of the building from which it operates; a student would mainly be concerned with the classroom or other areas in which their learning is undertaken, or in their room or dormitory if they reside at the school, college, etc.

You should not, however, ignore the remainder of the building, as it may affect the quality of the energy available to your part of the building. An analysis of it should be done to determine any energetic effects that need to be enhanced.

The elements of interest in a building would be:
• its shape;
• the construction materials used;
• its state of repair; and
• the consistency of its design with basic energetic principles.

These aspects are looked at more fully in Chapter 4.

General considerations

Feng Shui enhancements to a building's design and structure are often difficult and expensive. The main point of an examination of them is to determine whether there are any types of Feng Shui energetic impact that could be enhanced by other means, or for when you are deciding whether to select a particular building for use as a home, place of business or the location of other activity. If you are designing your own home or doing renovations, this analysis is also useful.

The opposite problem from 'shared' buildings is where your residence comprises more than one building. For instance, your house could have a separate garage, workshop or guest quarters; flats often have garages in separate parts of a building; businesses and schools may operate from a complex of buildings. In general terms, you need to analyse each building, or part of a building, separately. From the point of view of individuals, the larger structure (where most of the activities are carried out) will be the most important from a Feng Shui aspect. However, in the case of businesses and sport or education, where activities are carried out in a complex of buildings at the one location, determinations really require a Feng Shui consultant to cope with the many intricacies that may be involved.

The five elemental energy phases (discussed from pages 86 to 93) are more significant here than the eight energy conditions, which are better utilised in the 'room' component. *Ba gua* relationships are also applied to this environmental component. (Again, these aspects will be dealt with in detail in Chapter 4.)

The room component

Living creatures have organs which carry out the various functions necessary to sustain life. Buildings are quite similar, in that different areas are usually set aside for different activities. Rooms are often bounded by walls but do not need to be. Open-plan houses and offices may have distinct functional areas that are not separated by any physical barriers. When we talk of 'rooms' we are talking of functional areas.

Rooms, or functional areas, that you might consider in a house are:
- bedrooms;
- kitchen;
- bathroom;
- lounge;
- dining room;
- family area;
- storeroom;
- garage;
- laundry;
- foyer;
- hallway;
- study.

Functional areas of businesses would include:

- reception areas (physical, and mail and telephone communication areas);
- management offices/Boardroom;
- research and development areas;
- manufacturing and production areas;
- dispatch areas;
- conference and training areas;
- accounting and record-keeping areas (including computer processing and record-keeping locations);
- stock and storage areas; and
- staff amenity areas (kitchens, lunchrooms).

General considerations

When performing a Feng Shui analysis of rooms or functional areas, the focus is on ensuring that the energetic environment of these areas is good for the activities carried out in them. For instance, in a bedroom you wish to sleep. Now, let's say your personal energetic objective was to become more yang. If you were having difficulty getting to sleep or you were waking too easily — symptomatic of a too yang environment in the bedroom — you certainly would not want to make the bedroom environment more yang just to satisfy your personal energy objective. Rather select another room/area whose function is more consistent with your personal energy objective, for example, the living room.

Analysing rooms and functional areas will probably form the foundation of your Feng Shui activities. It is the easiest area in which to apply Feng Shui enhancements. The *ba gua* relationships can be applied at room level and the eight energy conditions are also a major Feng Shui tool here.

Furnishings and decorations component

Furnishings and decorations is an interesting area because it is actually how most of the Feng Shui enhancements are made. It includes tables, chairs, beds, baths, wardrobes, carpets, floor coverings, light fittings, curtains, blinds, pictures, ornaments, television sets, radios, computers, fish tanks, bird cages, indoor plants, fridges, washers, bookcases, log fires, gas appliances, air fresheners, photographs, mirrors, crystals, and so on.

Fortunately, we can break down the influence of all these items into the manner in which they influence the eight energy conditions. Therefore, when considering the purchase of a new item, there are basically eight questions that you need to ask about how that item will influence the yin/yang state of the energy conditions around it.

Considerations

Any comments made in this book about furnishings and decorations do not concern aesthetic qualities; they are about the energetic impact of the article in question. You *can* apply Feng Shui in a tasteful and artistic way and, in general, it works better that way. On the other hand, an article of great artistic merit may not be suitable for your Feng Shui. That's just the way it is!

The eight energy conditions

To make a proper assessment of whether you can control the energetic impact of an environment, or a component of an environment, you must have some idea of the nature of the changes it is possible to make to it. All changes to, or enhancements of, the environment can be classified as affecting one of the eight energy conditions. That is:

1 electromagnetic energy condition — light, colour and electrical fields;
2 sound energy condition — music, noise;
3 movement energy condition — of air and physical objects in the environment;
4 crystallised energy condition — as contained in physical objects, landforms, buildings, furniture and ornaments;
5 thermal energy condition — degree of heat and cold;
6 moisture energy condition — degree of wetness or dryness;
7 bio-energy condition — people, plants, animals, insects and fish; and
8 aroma energy condition — smells.

Electromagnetic energy

While we generally call this energy light, we now understand that the invisible spectrum is as important as the visible spectrum. Things such as ultraviolet light come immediately to mind. Less obvious are electric fields, microwaves and radio waves. These, along with light, are, however, simply part of the electromagnetic spectrum.

In assessing this energy condition we would look at:
- degree of visible light;
- degree of infra-red and ultraviolet light;
- frequency of visible light (colour);
- patterns of visible light (visual arts);
- intensity of electrical and magnetic fields; and
- intensity of microwave, radio wave, X-ray and other electromagnetic frequencies.

While we could get technical and use lots of sophisticated equipment to measure the electromagnetic frequencies that we can't see, we can also assess most of these quite easily with the few simple observations detailed below.

The visible spectrum

Most of us are already reasonable managers of visible light. When we build or buy our dwellings we take careful note of the number and size of windows and their exposure to the summer and winter sun; we put up curtains, blinds and awnings, and perhaps even arrange window tinting; for night-time or in poorly lit areas of the house we arrange artificial lighting. These can all be regarded as Feng Shui

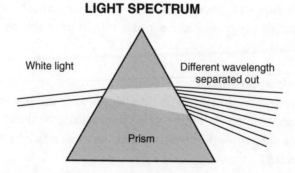

LIGHT SPECTRUM

White light

Different wavelength
separated out

Prism

techniques. They manage our environmental energy in respect of light.

In general, the more light there is, the more yang an environment will be. Flickering and regular abrupt changes in light, such as from the headlights of a stream of oncoming cars, or from a flashing neon sign are detrimental — including those from flashing Christmas tree lights!

bedroom more yang more light

Colour and the visual arts

Colour is a whole subject in itself and is dealt with in Chapter 4. Visual arts are also an important part of the energetic environment. Again, in the following comments on visual arts it is important to understand that Feng Shui professionals do not set themselves up as art critics. They are solely interested in the energetic, as opposed to the artistic. (The subject of paintings and photographs is dealt with in Chapter 4.)

Much art these days is abstract and non-representational. The brighter the colours, the more lines and angles, the more busy the picture is, the more yang its effects will be. The softer the colours, the more they merge and blend, the more lines curve and circle, the emptier the picture, the more its effects will be yin.

Any art which has a visual impact has an energetic effect that needs to be considered. This includes pottery and sculpture, which can be assessed in the same way as paintings and photographs. Not many of us immediately think of visual art when we think about computer games, television and video, but they do have an impact. Because the images are transitory their energetic impact is lessened, but if the same types of images are played for hours every day, their impact may be every bit as great as paintings. The images brought into our homes via these media (pictures of which we would not contemplate displaying) have a potential impact which we ignore at our own peril.

The invisible spectrum

Skin cancer and sunburn tell us how important the invisible spectrum can be. Also, don't you tend to feel just a little drained after coming back from a intense-light environment, such as a bright summer's day on the beach?

Excessive electromagnetic radiation (EMR)

It is unlikely we are going to be exposed to significant non-visible parts of the electromagnetic spectrum without visible signs of it. We must also remember the focus of the positive Feng Shui program is on improving the environment in which we live, not becoming paranoid about negative aspects of which we have previously been unaware!

Unless you are living directly beside an electrical power installation, under high-tension wires or right in front of a microwave dish, the most likely source of significant exposure to EMR is the visual display unit of computers. (The issue of mobile phones and heated water beds is dealt with in Appendix 1.) This is a bigger hazard than the television because we sit so close to it. The best solution is to use liquid crystal display (LCD) screens, as are currently found on notebook and laptop computers. This technology is different to cathode-ray tube displays and does not pose any EMR hazard. Otherwise, select an EMR-shielded VDU (which limits, but does not eliminate, the hazard). Also, make sure you sit as far away as you comfortably can from the screen and take frequent breaks away from it. Never sit close behind a cathode-ray tube in either a VDU or TV — the electromagnetic hazard there is higher than in front of the screen.

Computers and other electrical equipment generate heat. While this is not necessarily a problem in itself, when the equipment contains lots of plastics, the plastic is heated and tends to out-gas, that is, it releases toxins into the environment. EMR acts on the air to creates positive ions, which have a negative impact on our health and wellbeing. Make sure that any electrical equipment that feels warm and has plastic components operates in a well-ventilated area. Some varieties of plants are good at removing pollutants and positive ions (see Note 16, pages 208–9).

Another concern is where you sleep. Avoid having electrical equipment operating close to you, including such items as clock radios and electric blankets. Because of its polluting tendencies, the less electrical equipment in a bedroom the better. If you must watch television in bed (or play computer games), make sure that the room is well ventilated and, in this instance, consider having plants in the bedroom.

Unfortunately, in many houses, the power box is located on the exterior of a bedroom wall. If this is the case, do not put the head of the bed opposite the power box. If you have no choice but to have the bed in this position, consider moving it out from the wall and putting a thick wooden bedhead between you and the power box. For the internal bedroom walls, check that there are not major electrical appliances located on the other side of these walls. If you live in a high-rise development, particularly one with central airconditioning plants and elevators, it's worth finding out where the major power cables and electrical power equipment are located and siting your bed to minimise exposure.

If you are really worried about microwave and electrical installations being close by, get a professional reading done. Most likely you will find the levels to be only a small fraction of the accepted safety levels. It will also show you that it is the EMR fields you are generating with your equipment that are most likely to be your greatest concern. It's worth it to put your mind at rest.

One thing to keep firmly fixed in mind is that each of the eight environmental energy conditions can only be healthily adjusted within a limited range, and when making environmental changes, you must be careful not to create sha chi, si chi or stagnant chi conditions. For instance, electrical energy is very yang and if you wanted to increase the yang nature of an environment it would not be recommended that you do this by increasing the amount of electrical equipment in an environment, since this could too easily create sha chi. I am not suggesting you never buy an additional piece of electrical equipment; rather, that such purchases should not be made primarily as a means of enhancing the environmental energy.

Don't create an environment with too much or too little colour, that is too bright or too dim; with too much or too little electric or magnetic energy (yes, it is difficult, but possible, to have too little of these types of energy).

Sound energy

When we talk about sound we are talking about pressure waves. Some of these we hear, while others are pitched at either too high or too low a frequency for our ears to detect. It is supposedly the low-frequency pressure waves from a seismic disturbance (which travel faster than the higher-frequency audible sound waves) that alert birds and animals to earthquakes before humans hear and feel them.

It is important to remember that while the tympanic membranes of the ear are the most sensitive to sound, the whole body can actually 'hear' sound, since the pressure waves that make up sound pass through our bodies as well as through the air around us.

Audible sound

The first thing most people think of when they consider audible sound is volume. We all know how difficult it can be to concentrate when sound levels are too high. This is an excess sound chi condition. However, if you have ever experienced absolute quiet, such as you might find deep in a dry cave, this might pose a problem too, with the slightest sound made distracting you. This is a deficient sound Chi condition.

Noise levels can be a health problem and certain levels are mandated as hazardous. Even lower levels can disrupt sleep and concentrated activity. Cars are amazingly noisy, particularly tyre noise on high-speed highways. Airway flight paths are also a problem.

Quantity of sound is not the only important thing, consistency and quality of sound are also worth considering. Sudden, sharp sounds, such as the screech of brakes, the squeal of tyres and the honking of horns, have a stressful effect on our physical body and a disruptive effect on our thinking processes.

Fortunately, sounds can be reflected, absorbed or masked, which gives us a number of Feng Shui management techniques. A solid, unbroken surface tends to reflect sound. Thus, if we want to maintain sound levels, we can use plastic and gloss paint surfaces and varnished tiles or wood. Broken, irregular surfaces, such as those found in many types of cloth, help absorb sound and scatter it. Wind blowing through leaves and vegetation, and water splashing over rocks both create a jumble of sound known as 'white noise'. Not only is this noise beneficial in its impact but other, less pleasant sounds get lost within it.

Music and other sounds

Playing music is another way of creating a beneficial sound environment. (For more on music, see Chapter 4.) Other sounds, such as some birdsong (definitely not the sound of cockatoos!), bells and wind chimes can create pleasant, beneficial sound.

Inaudible sound

Machinery and electrical equipment can emit sound that is either at too high or too low a pitch for the human ear to detect. Both of these can have a negative impact. Watch for vibration. If the ground or building has a vibration, then this may indicate inaudible sound.

Is it possible to get a stagnant chi condition with sound? This occurs with a dull, repetitive sound, which seems to dominate the sound environment, making it all that we hear. Each individual sound is unremarkable but its continual repetition can be exasperating. Think of the effect of a dripping tap.

Movement energy

Movement requires energy; the nature of movement reflects the energy involved. While movement is yang compared to stillness, the faster the movement, the more yang it becomes. Also, when movement is angular and changeable, it is seen as more yang than when compared to smooth, slow movement.

Wind is an obvious form of moving energy. A light breeze can be most beneficial but strong winds can lead to excess chi. Utter stillness is a problem, leading to deficient chi conditions. Airconditioning, fans and other ventilation devices are simply forms of artificial wind and can be assessed as such.

Movement goes beyond just air movement. Water movement also has significant impact on the state of chi. Large waterfalls, rapids, stormy oceans and rivers in spate can all generate excess chi; still water can lead to chi stagnation. (Lakes and ponds often have significant currents that move the water around internally, thus avoiding stagnant chi. Such currents can be caused by thermal convection or by movement of groundwater).

Movement of physical objects, including that of the leaves and branches of plants, and movement of animals and people, affect environmental chi. Movements at railway stations, shopping centres and road systems can be so significant as to result in the creation of excessive chi. The more movement, the faster the movement, the more yang it is.

Fountains, mobiles, windmills, fish, birds and pets can all be used to increase the amount of movement energy in an environment.

Crystallised energy ('energy of form')

The more that we learn about the universe, the easier it is to start seeing it in terms of energy rather than matter. Consider, for instance, the 'standing waves' of water that most of us have seen in streams and other fast-flowing water. These waves differ from normal ocean waves in that the wave itself stays in one place while the water moves through it. (In normal ocean waves, the waves move across the surface, though the actual water that forms them merely rises and falls.) Such standing waves of water are caused by currents of water being deflected from objects on the bottom of the stream or river. They seem to have a real physical existence but are in fact only a pattern of moving water. Atoms, the building blocks which make up all the physical objects which surround us, have a similar nature. There is nothing 'solid' at the core of an atom; it can also be regarded as simply a permanent pattern of flowing energy. For this reason we will use the term 'crystallised' energy when referring to physical objects. 'Crystallised energy' is used to reflect the fact that matter is energy which has a pattern or structure.

In terms of shape and texture, the yin/yang impact of physical objects is as follows:

lesser yang
- basic shape is columnar
- surface is ridged, or rough and abrasive

greater yang
- basic shape is conical or pyramidal
- surface has sharp edges and points

lesser yin
- basic shape is hemispherical
- surface may be bumpy but without points

greater yin
- basic shape is irregular, may have holes or spaces
- surface is smooth and slick.

Excess amounts of matter can create excessive chi effects. Having large, heavy beams on a ceiling, living in a small building dominated by a large building on either side, or placing a rock 20 metres high by 5 metres in diameter in an average front garden are just a few examples of this. Having a quarry in front of your house might create

79

a deficient chi effect, a large decaying tree in your front garden may create a stagnant chi effect.

Straight lines and sharp objects

Some Feng Shui writers work themselves up into a passion about straight lines and sharp objects, predicting doom and destruction wherever such articles are found. Straight lines are not natural, they say! Spiky plants or leaves with points are bad Feng Shui!

However, if we look around us, we can see that nature is full of straight lines, from the tessellated lines in rock platforms often found at ocean edges, to the upward, straight lines of many tree trunks. What amazes me is that the most common Feng Shui remedy is crystals, which are just brimful of sharp, straight lines.

I am the first to agree that too many straight lines or sharp edges are going to create excessive chi but, in a low-energy environment, a few straight, sharp lines might be just what the doctor ordered (or at least what these same writers ordered when they told you to go and get a crystal!). So let's not get too worked up about straight lines per se.

How about sharp, pointed objects? Was the cactus nature's mistake, along with thousands of other spiky, thorny plants and animals? Has the cactus ruined the earth's Feng Shui? What about the rose? It's all a question of degree. If your sharp, pointed objects are a physical hazard or psychologically threatening, then, from a Feng Shui aspect, it probably is time to do something about them.

One of my Feng Shui consultants performed a little experiment. He loves cacti and had the whole front border of his garden bristling with them. However, he had few visitors to his house and wondered whether it might be something to do with the nature of the chi that these cacti were generating. Rather than toss them out he moved them to a less visible portion of the garden. Almost immediately, friends he had known for over ten years who were always 'going to drop in' turned up on the doorstep. As the cacti are still alive and kicking, it was obviously the original positioning on the fire side of the property that was the problem.

The message here is twofold. First, don't panic about negative Feng Shui connotations. Most things can have good and bad effects, depending on your energy objectives. Second, perform your own

Feng Shui experiments on an incremental basis. Don't start off by rebuilding your whole house. Look for smaller, easily made changes and then see what happens.

Thermal energy

Thermal energy seems a nice, easy energy condition to work with because we all know when something is hotter or colder than something else — it's just a matter of using a thermometer. In fact, besides their actual temperature, things can seem colder or hotter depending on the relative thermal conductivity of two objects. Thermal conductivity is the speed with which thermal energy moves into or out of a substance. Place a metal can and a dry piece of cloth into the freezer for a couple of hours. Both will come out the same temperature, but the metal will feel a lot colder! Thus using carpets instead of tiles can reduce the impact of temperature differences, and it is the energetic impact that changes Feng Shui.

The hotter something seems when compared with something else, the more yang it is in respect of that other object; the colder it seems, the more yin.

The regulation of heat and cold was probably humankind's first real attempt to manage its energetic environment. The wearing of clothes is primarily a heat management technique, as witnessed by the fact that clothes are often dispensed with in hot climates but very rarely dispensed with in cold climates!

Wood, gas and electric fires, fans, air coolers and conditioners are all obvious ways in which we regulate heat. Less obvious are ventilation techniques, heat sinks, construction materials, etc. Changes to thermal energy can have one of the fastest impacts on our Feng Shui.

The natural assumption is that the warmer the environment, the more energetic its impact will be; the colder the environment, the more yin its effects. So why do we feel more awake in cold conditions and sleepy in warm environments? When using thermal energy, we need to be aware of how our bodies work. The human body is a homeostatic system that seeks balance. If our internal core temperature rises too high, the body responds by making us sleepy and lethargic, thus less likely to generate metabolic heat from activity. On the other hand, if our core temperature starts to fall, our body makes us alert and active so that we generate heat through muscular activity, even initiating shivering to raise body heat.

Of course, the body can only maintain homeostasis within limits. If the core temperature gets too hot then we die, no matter how little we move. If the core temperature gets too low, we get sleepy again, as our metabolism shuts down and we die. Such extremes of heat and cold can be regarded as sha chi and si chi conditions, respectively.

Since what we are interested in is the temperature of our bodies, we should first try to adjust that temperature by adjusting the clothes we wear. It is wasteful (and expensive) to heat or cool a whole environment when all we need to do is wear warmer or cooler clothing. Heating is also more efficient when you use such things as underfloor heating, rather than the traditional wood and electric fires.

Moisture energy

Moisture refers not to the state of being liquid but to containing H_2O. For example, solid moisture = ice; liquid moisture = water; gaseous moisture = steam. The degree to which an environment contains any of these substances is the degree to which it is moist or dry.

The state of a liquid is sometimes confused with its yin nature. Water wearing away rock is seen as yin overcoming yang, when what is being referred to is actually the soft, non-resisting and yielding yin aspects of water as a liquid. Any liquid, in comparison to its solid form is, in fact, yang — if made more yin it becomes a solid; if made more yang it becomes a gas. (There is, for instance, nothing yin-like in lava's influence on most things, yet lava is, after all, only liquid rock.)

Remember our earlier discussion, when I talked about the dangers of believing that objects were yin or yang in themselves rather than relative to each other? This is an example of how important that is. When we talk about moisture we are talking about 'water' energy nature, not 'liquid' energy nature.

It sometimes surprises people that water is seen by the Chinese as an energy. However, even in modern science, water plays a very special role. It is difficult to see how life on earth could have begun without water. How would complex chemicals have had the opportunity to mix and form self-replicating chemicals, such as DNA? Once these replicating chemicals formed, how would they have survived the harsh environment without their protective bath of water? Water, indeed, gave birth to and nurtured life — an ultimate yin characteristic.

Water always seeks the lowest point. This is not true of steam, or even mist, so this should not be seen as a characteristic of moisture. Clouds are formed from evaporated water, thus it is the water (or should we really say 'moisture') cycle that supports life on earth.

H_2O can be in its water form, moving downwards, and still have a yang effect, such as in a waterfall. This is because the movement aspect of water can override water's basic nature. A tropical rainstorm might also be seen as yang, whereas a soft spring shower might be yin. Temperature plays a large role as well. One must therefore be quite alert in assessing the yin or yang impact of water other than the drier/yang, wetter/yin evaluation.

Putting moisture in your environment does not mean paddling around in puddles of water. Look first at the air in your environment and how humid it is before deciding on the materials to be used. Ceramics and plastics will tend to be drier than woods and fabrics. Changing the balance of these materials changes the moisture levels of the environment. The use of plants, aquariums and fountains are obvious ways to increase moisture.

Remember, you should always be working with balance in mind. Deciding you are too yang and turning your back garden into a bog (stagnant chi) or having dozens of waterfalls and fountains (excessive chi) is just as bad as deciding you are too yin and turning your home environment into a desert.

Bio-energy

Living things, be they plants, animals or human beings, are part of our environment's energetic influence. The more similar an animal is to a human being, the closer its energy needs will tend to be. It is therefore a good sign if your garden is regularly visited by warm-blooded wildlife such as birds and mammals. Not only do these visitors make their own contribution to the energetic environment but their presence indicates that they find the environment benign and attractive, which is a good indicator of its energetic quality.

It is a little difficult to attract much wildlife (apart from birds) in the city. Therefore, one reason to have a pet is the positive bio-energy it provides. It is relatively common knowledge that, as a group, people who keep pets have longer life spans than people who don't. Keeping virtually any pet is beneficial from a Feng Shui perspective, though the energies of some pets will be more in tune with one person's energy than another.

In decreasing order of yang effects are mammals, birds, reptiles, fish and insects (I do know of people who keep spiders as pets!). Dogs, as a whole, are more yang than cats but I have seen some fairly yin dogs and some very yang cats. The nature and personality of your pet is usually self-evident.

Infestations of rats, mice, frogs, toads and insects is another matter. Even large numbers of mammals such as cats and dogs can have negative implications. One or two members of other species can help balance energy — too many unbalance it. You might think you could never have enough birds, but anyone who has had a flock of cockatoos as regular visitors would give you a different opinion!

Excessive chi exists when there is too much bio-energy. Having a dozen cats and dogs or turning your house into an indoor jungle with plants and aquaria can create this effect. On the other hand, a place with no plants or animals and few people will be deficient in chi. Infestations of insects and rodents are often associated with stagnant chi. A well-ventilated, clutter- and garbage-free environment will rarely attract such pests. There are special conditions for farms and buildings in undeveloped areas, as the pests may overflow from areas of stagnant chi in close proximity to the building. This can include city buildings close to drainage systems that have stagnant chi.

Do pets have Feng Shui?
Another way of asking this question is: 'Are pets influenced by environmental energy?' The obvious answer to this question is 'Yes'. The same logic applies as does to human beings. The energy influence will be most strong for wherever the pet spends most of its time — its kennel, sleeping basket or in front of the food bowl!

You might think *ba gua* is not important, but if you and your animal are having 'relationship' problems then you might look to see what you can do to improve this energy. Similarly, look at the animal's 'career'. Your pet's 'career' or 'mission' might include such things as protecting you, providing companionship, being an object of beauty or even winning competitions. If any of these are not working out, you might try making Feng Shui changes on exactly the same basis as you would for yourself, but focusing on areas where your pet spends most of its time.

Acupressure and acupuncture are being increasingly used on racehorses. One wonders how long it will be before Feng Shui principles are applied to their stalls!

Aroma energy

Perhaps because flowers can be one of the first images that spring to mind when we think of 'aroma', we constantly underestimate the power of this energy. This is curious because perhaps the last house you would buy is one with an aroma you did not like. It is also interesting to speculate on just how much of the initial attraction between people is due to smell. The chemicals that we smell in this instance are called pheromones. Human beings' aroma-sensing system is hardwired into the most primitive part of the human brain, situated immediately on top of the spinal cord and often referred to as the 'reptilian' part of the brain, the one that is most likely to stimulate a reaction from us before the conscious mind even knows what is going on.

On analysis, a smell is simply a molecule released from another object. I find it fascinating, however, that flowers, which exist to attract various insects and animals in order that they can be pollinated, issue scent molecules which humans also find attractive. There seems little evolutionary advantage in humans being attracted to the smell of a rose, yet I know of no fruit, nut or other edible object that elicits the same feelings as the rose's aroma.

On the other hand, smells resulting from decay disgust us, which would seem to have a negative evolutionary advantage. Many animals eaten by humans are, in fact, scavengers who live off dead animals. If our ancient hunter–gatherer ancestors had been attracted by smells of decay, then they would have been likely to remain in the same area as the decaying carcasses of dead animals. This would also have kept them in the same area as a potential food source — the scavengers that feed off such carcasses.

The smells of some flowers (such as that of lavender) initiate the relaxation response, while other smells (such as that of smelling salts) stimulate and raise consciousness. Holding your nose may prevent you from 'smelling' a particular scent but it does not prevent the impact of it on the body, as the skin also absorbs aroma molecules.

I would argue that 'taste' is just another aspect of 'smell', as both senses relate to detecting the nature of a substance through the sampling of its released molecules. In the case of smell, these are airborne molecules; in the case of taste, the molecules are still attached to the substance. We often confuse what is smelled and what is tasted. Think how tasteless food becomes when you have a cold and cannot smell! Babies, of course, learn lots about their environment by tasting it, constantly putting things in their mouths.

Just as there are some wavelengths of light we cannot see and some wavelengths of sound we cannot hear, there are also some molecules we cannot taste or smell. However, this does not mean that these substances cannot have an effect on us. A new house, a newly manufactured article or an industrial area may contain molecules that we would be better off being able to smell. We will look further at how to manage our aroma environment in Chapter 4.

The five elemental energy phases

The five elemental energy phases are sometimes called the five elements, due to a mistaken comparison with the four elements in ancient Western philosophy (also, I suspect, because 'five elements' is less of a mouthful!). There is, in fact, no relationship whatsoever between the two theories. What the ancient Chinese were referring to were their observations of nature that disclosed an internal rhythm, pulse or cycle in the chi energy that powered all activity.

The five elemental energy phases are:
• wood nature;
• fire nature;
• metal nature;
• water nature;
• earth nature.

Just as we can understand the yin/yang nature of the relationship between the individual and their environment and adjust that environment to maximise the health of the individual in terms of the eight major life activities, so, too, can we understand the five elemental energy phases nature of the individual and their environment and adjust that environment, with similar benefits.

One common misunderstanding about the five elemental energy phases is that a person's attributed birth element is all we have to worry about when looking at the energy nature of that person's required environment. This is tantamount to saying that if a person is born with a yin or yang nature, we can tell the environment they require from that simple fact only.

You need to recognise that the elemental energy phases are continuous; thus, the energy needs of a person born ten minutes before the start of spring and a person born ten minutes afterwards would not be nearly as different as the energy needs of a person born on the first day of spring and those of a person born on the last day (even though the former would be water and wood types, while the latter would both be categorised as wood). So don't worry about whether you need to take daylight saving into account when working out your element!

The five elemental energy phases theory is even more sophisticated than yin/yang theory, in that each of the energy phases has a particular influence on a set of organ meridians, internal viscera and aspects of the psyche. Indeed, when working with this theory, it is sometimes difficult to say where Feng Shui finishes and traditional Chinese medicine begins.

Note 2 on compass directions (see page 180–87) shows how the human desire to represent nature with neat, two-dimensional, diagrammatic representations can lead to misunderstandings about

ENERGY PHASE	RELATED ORGAN MERIDIAN	RELATED ELEMENT OF PSYCHE
WOOD	Liver	Hun
FIRE	Heart	Shen
METAL	Lungs	P'o
WATER	Kidney	Chi
EARTH	Spleen	I

the nature of direction. The same problem exists with diagrammatic representations of the five elemental energy phases, when the relationship between the five elements is drawn as a neat little pentagram (see below).

This diagram makes it easy to show the various controlling and reinforcing relationships between the energy phases. The trouble is, when we come to relate this diagram to the seasons of nature, for instance, we end up one season short. What should we do? The typical approach is to create another season, such as high summer. A little bit more forced reasoning and we can relate earth nature energy to high summer because 'We get fires late in late summer and these turn trees into ash, which represents earth.' The fact that we then have seasons of unequal lengths and lose the one-to-one relationship between the yin/yang phases and the seasons is overlooked.

The ancient Chinese did not have five seasons. Earth nature is not, in fact, a synonym for soil nature but a reference to the grounding nature of the planet as a whole. The earth energy phase was seen as different from the others, with older diagrams showing not a pentagram but a circle of four energy phases around the central energy phase of earth nature.

NORMAL REPRESENTATION OF THE FIVE ELEMENTS

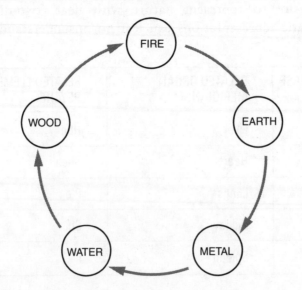

If we follow this older approach we can then say:
- WOOD = SPRING = lesser yang
- FIRE = SUMMER = greater yang
- METAL = AUTUMN = lesser yin
- WATER = WINTER = greater yin

The earth is the 'grounder' of seasons. Before we can have spring, summer, autumn and winter, the earth must experience a seasonal cycle. It is the revolution of the earth on its tilted axis as it orbits the sun that creates the seasons. Thus, it is the grounding force of gravity that is the prime agent for our experience of the changing seasons. It brings each one to a conclusion and starts the next. In this sense, earth is yin in respect of all the other elemental energy phases, although when comparing its interaction with other energy phases it supports the basic nature of each energy phase. (When you look at the sine wave diagram on page 91, you will see that wood and fire are on the rising yang side of the wave, giving these elements a basic yang nature, and metal and water are on the falling side of the wave, giving these a basic yin nature).

ANCIENT CHINESE VIEW OF THE FIVE ELEMENTS

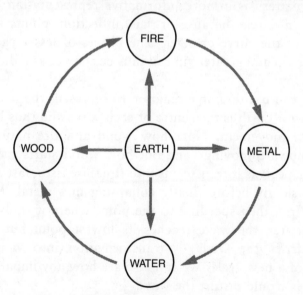

This is not as 'tidy' in diagrammatic form but it provides us much more to work with. For instance, when looking at an individual from the five elemental energy phases viewpoint (regardless of whether a person is born in a fire year, water year or whatever) it is first important to make sure of the earth nature energy and that the person is properly grounded, in order to have a firm energetic foundation. This is one of the reasons the Chinese favour a square (earth nature) design for a house or room. If the foundation shape is not correct, energies may be out of balance.

We can probably go one better than the ancient Chinese in representing the five elements, due to the fact we have had a chance to learn things the Chinese did not know, one of these being the 'wave' nature of the universe. Sine waves reveal to us that, in the real world, cycles are not circular. A cycle may repeat itself but it does not start and finish in the same place in terms of space/time. (Modern physics regards space and time as an inseparable, unified whole.) For instance, the earth goes through a cycle of seasons but it does not return to the same physical location on 1 January each year. The earth circles the sun and the sun has moved a long way through space during that year, as the solar system orbits the galactic centre and the galaxy itself moves through space (at quite astonishing speeds, I might add!).

A wave pattern is a more informative representation of yin and yang than a circle because it has inflection points where the 'direction' of the curve changes. The phases of lesser yang, greater yang, lesser yin and greater yin can thus be shown, as indicated in the diagram below.

Now we can use the same diagram to represent the five elemental energy phases. Earth is the centre of each wave and thus has its own direction of movement. Note how wood and fire nature energies represent upward-moving yang but how wood starts rising slowly, reaching its peak as it transforms into fire. Fire rises, fast at first, but ever more slowly before finally collapsing into metal. Metal falls, slowly at first, then speeding to the point where it transforms into water. In water, the wave reaches its lowest point but its rate of slowing carries the seeds of transformation into yang and the beginning of a new cycle. We can also see how any imbalance of the five energies would distort the wave.

YIN–YANG RELATIONSHIP'S SINE WAVE

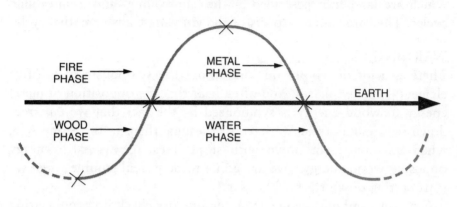

$\times$ = INFLECTION POINTS

From an analysis of the above diagram, we now ought to be able to predict the impact of various phases of energy on each other from a yin/yang perspective, as shown in the table below.

ELEMENT	WOOD	FIRE	METAL	WATER	EARTH
WOOD	Yang	Yang	Yang	Yang	Yang
FIRE	Yang	Yang	Yang	Yang	Yang
METAL	Yin	Yin	Yin	Yin	Yin
WATER	Yin	Yin	Yin	Yin	Yin
EARTH	Yin	Yin	Yang	Yang	Yin

To use the table: read from the top row of elements (the current energy state of the environment) then go across to the left-hand column to find the element you wish to add. You can then see the overall yin/yang effect on the energetics of the system. If you want to find an element with a yin or yang effect on another particular element, select that element from the top row, and then find which elements will create the desired effect.

This is the real meaning of the 'creative' and 'destructive' cycles, which are far better described as the 'controlling' and 'reinforcing' cycles. They are simply aspects of the yin/yang transformative cycle.

WARNING!!

There is a lot of woolly thinking about the symbolism of the five elemental energy phases. You often hear that the opposition of metal energy to wood energy is symbolised by the fact that we cut trees down with metal axes! We have to presume then, in the Stone Age, when trees were cut down with stone axes, it was earth energy opposing wood energy. (We are going to be in real trouble when we start cutting down trees with lasers!)

Give any symbolism you encounter a reality check, to avoid getting misled. Remember, the whole point of symbolism is to allow us to understand the nature of the particular phase of the energy so that we will know how it behaves.

Description of the five elemental energy phases

The intention here is only to provide a working knowledge of the five elemental energy phases in so far as it is required for the positive Feng Shui program. Thus, only a brief description of each of these phases has been given.

Wood nature energy

Wood nature should not be misunderstood as 'timber' nature. Instead, it refers to 'tree' nature and symbolises growth and expansion. In applying it to the seasons, wood nature energy is spring. It is lesser yang.

Fire nature energy

The nature of fire is to consume and change things. It is a symbol of transformation. Fire energy is thus related to yang. In applying it to the seasons, fire nature energy is summer. Because extreme yang is the beginning of yin, fire nature energy is also the beginning of the second half of the cycle.

Metal nature energy

The nature of metal is one of the more difficult energies to understand. Metal is distillation, purification and concentration. A metal must be refined from an ore. Metal nature energy is lesser yin and is associated with autumn, a time of harvest.

Water nature energy
The nature of water is to be fluid and formless, always to seek the lowest point; the water energy phase is thus related to yin. In applying it to the seasons, water nature energy is winter. Because yin creates yang, water nature energy is also the period of rebirth, the start of a new cycle.

Earth nature energy
The nature of earth is grounding or centralising. It is yin because it moves towards the centre, aggregates and concentrates. In comparison to earth, all other energy phases are yang. Earth nature is associated with all seasons rather than a particular season. At one time, the ancient Chinese used to allocate the last ten days of each of the four seasons as relating to earth. This represented the role of centralising energy in transforming one season into another.

Some final thoughts before you are on your way

Recognise that your life is highly individual. The time and resources you wish to commit to Feng Shui may also vary substantially from what others can or will commit to it. Both to accommodate this and to take advantage of the flexibility of possible approaches, the positive Feng Shui program has been constructed from a series of modules from which you can select *what you need*; you decide on which components of which environments you are going to work. This allows you to personalise your own program by selecting the modules appropriate to your needs and interests, and to carry it out at your own pace.

You are now ready to complete the second step in the positive Feng Shui program.

Form 2 — Identification of significant environments

ENVIRONMENT	MODULES	YES/NO
HOME Average weekly hours _60_ Include in program? _____	Local environment Land and garden Buildings Rooms Fixtures and fittings	_____ _____ _____ _____ _____
WORKPLACE Average weekly hours _20_ Include in program? _____	Local environment Land and garden Buildings Rooms Fixtures and fittings	_____ _____ _____ _____ _____
STUDY LOCATION Average weekly hours _10-8_ Include in program? _____	Local environment Land and garden Buildings Rooms Fixtures and fittings	_____ _____ _____ _____ _____
RELIGIOUS ACTIVITY LOCATION Average weekly hours _0_ Include in program? _____	Local environment Land and garden Buildings Rooms Fixtures and fittings	_____ _____ _____ _____ _____
TRAINING, SPORTING OR EXERCISE AREA Average weekly hours _10_ Include in program? _____	Local environment Land and garden Buildings Rooms Fixtures and fittings	_____ _____ _____ _____ _____

ENVIRONMENT	MODULES	YES/NO
SOCIAL OR RECREATION AREA Average weekly hours _____ Include in program? _____	Local environment Land and garden Buildings Rooms Fixtures and fittings	_____ _____ _____ _____ _____

Chapter 4

The Positive Feng Shui
Program in Action

Introduction

Having gained a working knowledge of the concepts underlying Feng Shui, as well as identified your personal energy objectives, you are now ready to start making beneficial changes to your Feng Shui. All changes are achieved by altering one or more of the eight environmental energies mentioned in Chapter 3:

• electromagnetic;
• sound;
• movement;
• crystallised;
• thermal;
• moisture;
• bio-energy; and
• aroma.

With each of these the following approaches need to be taken:
• Identify and eliminate any excess chi, deficient chi and stagnant chi conditions that may relate to the particular energy condition.
• Work on personal energy objectives by selecting appropriate Feng Shui enhancement techniques (making sure that these enhancements are not 'overdone', thereby further creating the conditions you are trying to eliminate).

It is suggested that you first read through this chapter, identifying any excess, deficient or stagnant chi conditions in your environments. These should be noted on Form 3 on page 174, along with a proposed solution selected from those supplied in the tables entitled 'Eliminating excess, deficient and stagnant chi conditions', which appear throughout this chapter.

You will generally get more benefit from rectifying any sha chi, si chi and stagnant chi conditions that you have detected than you will from modifying the yin/yang influence of various environmental energy conditions. It therefore makes sense that you should resolve as many of these conditions as you can before moving on to the remainder of the program. However, be sure to remember that you should view any adverse energy situations that you find not as threats, but as opportunities to shift your overall energy balance positively.

Once you are ready to move on to the next stage of the program, select the most important of your energy objectives and work through each environmental energy area, noting your proposed Feng Shui solutions on Form 4 (located on page 177).

In making this selection, keep in mind that a Feng Shui enhancement technique works in one of the following ways:

- increasing/decreasing the amount of energy entering your environment;
- increasing/decreasing the circulation of existing energy within your environment;
- increasing/decreasing the quantity of energy created within your environment; or
- increasing the overall quality of the energy.

To get the most effective results from your Feng Shui program when you have a choice between Feng Shui enhancement techniques, apply them in the following order.

For a more yang effect
When seeking to create a more yang effect from an environmental energy, apply:
- firstly, those techniques that increase the amount of the energy in question entering the environment;

- then, those techniques that increase the circulation of the existing energy; and
- finally, those techniques that increase the generation of energy within the environment.

For a more yin effect
When seeking to create a more yin effect from an environmental energy, apply:
- firstly, those techniques that decrease the generation of energy in question within the environment;
- then, those techniques that decrease the amount of the energy entering the environment; and
- finally those techniques that increase the circulation of the existing energy.

Points to keep in mind
- Too much chi is as bad as too little — you are seeking balance.
- Avoid trying too many enhancement techniques at the one time.
- Chi can never be experienced directly. What you are doing is adjusting the underlying nature of chi.

We will also look at special considerations that apply to different components of your environment, such as the nature and function of buildings/rooms and the energetic impact of the local environment.

Electromagnetic energy enhancement techniques

As already discussed in Chapter 3, the energy of the electromagnetic spectrum is experienced in a number of ways, depending on the frequency of the energy. Because of this, it is easier to focus your enhancement techniques by considering electromagnetic energy from the following perspectives:
- light;
- colour;
- electromagnetic radiation and fields; and
- visual arts and symbols.

Mirrors and crystals are such important tools for enhancing light energy that they have been given their own sections.

Light
Background
Here we are dealing with the quantity or intensity of light found within an environment, whether received naturally from the sun or generated artificially.

Identifying excess, deficient and stagnant chi conditions
Excess chi conditions of light can be identified in situations when light intensity is sufficient to cause conditions such as sunburn and light-related headaches. It is also present in cold climates, such as those in which snow-blindness occurs, and needs to be watched for in any environment where there is significant reflection of light, as from water, sand and glass. Look out for large glass buildings, unpainted or silver-painted roofs, solar panel installations and car parks (which can contain hectares of highly reflective metal and glass).

Deficient chi conditions occur where there is an insufficient quantity of light. This does not just mean that you get eyestrain trying to do close work. Modern medicine has identified Seasonally Affective Disorder, or SAD, syndrome that occurs as light intensity and duration falls during the autumn and winter months and the consequent negative impact on the physical and psychological health of individuals. Our bodies also require sunlight for proper metabolic activity, such as the synthesis of Vitamin D.

In deciding whether you have a si chi condition in respect of light and your health, you have to consider all environments. Your home may be low in light, but if you work outside all day this should not be a problem from the viewpoint of your health; however, there may still be other valid Feng Shui reasons to increase the yang nature of your home light environment.

It is unusual to get stagnant chi conditions occurring with light unless you have an artificial light environment where there is no variation in light intensity over a long period of time.

Creating a 'controllable' light environment
When planning a garden or designing a house, it never hurts to build in some elements of control. Some ways of doing this are as follows:
- Trees and vegetation close to windows and other points of light entry should be pot-based, enabling them to be easily moved.

(This can also be an advantage in bushfire-risk areas, where such vegetation can be quickly moved from close proximity to the dwelling.)

- It is always better to make windows larger than strictly necessary. It is relatively easy to reduce the light coming through windows but difficult to increase it.
- Include current control devices on lights, allowing control of brightness to the level required.
- Have the lighting in a room come from several sources — only the number or lights required will then need to be turned on.

Remember to take account of the different levels of light received by your property in different seasons. If there is a problem with low levels of light in the winter, then consider having either deciduous trees or pot-based trees and plants. The latter can be moved elsewhere during winter but provide needed shade in summer. If the problem is high levels of light in the summer, the solution is the same.

You might also remember that it is the condition of the light energy while you are actually present that is most important. If you are only ever at home when it is dark, then it is the light condition at this time that is important; if you rise and sleep according to the position of the sun, then the artificial light condition at night is not going to be all that significant.

Adjusting the 'internal circulation' of light
When a photon (smallest unit of light) hits a surface, it is either absorbed or reflected. (We will disregard, for the moment, the changes in frequency that can occur, as this makes no difference to the recommendations made below.) The quantity of light in circulation is thus the light energy entering the room, less that absorbed into the various objects in the room. All surfaces absorb some light, so the more the surface area of a room is increased, the more the light circulated is reduced. A rough surface can have many times the surface area of a flat surface, so rough-finish paints and renders tend to be quite absorptive. Rough surfaces can still look and feel soft, as with silk and matt paint finishes.

Adjusting the 'quality' of artificial illumination
Artificial illumination can come from combustion, as with gaslight, firelight and candlelight. The light from these sources tends to have

a beneficial quality. There are problems with the spectra produced by electric lights, particularly fluorescent ones; therefore it is strongly recommended that you try to get as much of any artificial light as possible from either combustion or full-spectrum electric lights, the latter emitting frequencies that more closely match natural sunlight. (These are available at any lighting shop — just specify what you want at the time of purchase.)

Because televisions and computer screens are used for other purposes, we do not often think of them in terms of artificial light sources, yet, particularly in the case of the television, they are, often for hours at a time, the major source of light in a room. It is preferable to have other healthier light sources in a room while you are watching television and using a computer.

Not all activities require electric light. You might, for instance, consider bathing by candlelight! For those wanting to improve their personal relationships, here is an interesting fact. When we look at someone's face, small pupils are interpreted as lack of interest or hostility, whereas larger pupils are seen as expressing interest in and concern for us. The lower the light level (as long as you can still clearly see the other person's eyes!), the larger the pupil dilates. This is why we see softly lit restaurants as romantic places.

Symbols
Different qualities of light can be symbolised in drawings, paintings and photographs, etc. This can vary from the strong, bright light seen in pictures of the Greek Islands, to evening scenes of the European countryside depicting the soft, dappled light found there. You can, of course, use pictures of candlelit or firelight scenes, light through early morning mist, gaslight and many other scenes to evoke certain energetic qualities of light.

Colour
Background
Colour is the name we give both to our visual experience of an object and to the property of light that can be described in terms of the spectral characteristics of the light emitted, reflected or transmitted by an object.

Colour is an important indicator of the energy of a living environment and is often relatively easy to control. A considerable

Table 1 — Eliminating excess chi, deficient chi and stagnant chi conditions associated with light

ENERGY PROBLEM	ENERGY SOLUTION (ENHANCEMENT)	COMMENTS
EXCESS CHI	• Establish light barriers that reduce light entering property. • Reduce the number of reflective materials on your land or property. • Increase use of absorptive materials. • Reduce artificial illumination.	Light barriers can be: • fences, bushes and trees around a property; awnings, verandahs, blinds, 'solar guard' tinting on windows, even leadlighting. Reflective materials include mirrors, polished and high-gloss surfaces, glass and crystal, metallic surfaces and ceramics. Absorptive materials include rough surfaces, matt finishes on paints, use of fabrics rather than plastics and vinyls. This can be done by: • turning on only as many lights as are necessary and only when necessary; reducing the wattage of light bulbs; using shades and filters with artificial illumination.
DEFICIENT CHI	• Remove light barriers that reduce light entering the property. • Increase the number of reflective materials on your land or property. • Decrease use of absorptive materials • Increase artificial illumination.	Light barriers can be: • fences, bushes and trees around a property; awnings, verandahs, blinds, 'solar guard' tinting on windows, even leadlighting. Reflective materials include mirrors, polished and high-gloss surfaces, glass and crystal, metallic surfaces and ceramics. Absorptive materials include rough surfaces, matt finishes on paints, use plastics and vinyls rather than fabrics. This can be done by: • increasing the number of lights and the period that they are on; increasing the wattage of existing lights; using lighter shades and filters with artificial illumination.
STAGNANT CHI	• Increase reflective surfaces. • Vary light intensity.	These include mirrors, polished and high-gloss surfaces, glass and crystal, metallic surfaces and ceramics.

Table 2 — Adjusting light energy in accordance with personal energy objectives

ENERGY OBJECTIVE	ENERGY SOLUTION (ENHANCEMENT)	COMMENTS
INCREASE YANG	• Increase sources and intensity of light.	This can be done by: • installation of additional or larger windows and skylights; • removal of awnings, external blinds and shutters, as well as trees and bushes causing shade; • making sure that curtains and blinds do not detract from window space when in open position; • installation of additional artificial light sources or increasing wattage of bulbs (not above specification for light fitting); • replacement of lampshades and light fittings that block or absorb large quantities of light emitted.
DECREASE YANG	• Decrease sources and intensity of light.	This can be done by: • removal or blocking off of windows and skylights; • addition of awnings, external blinds and shutters, along with planting trees and bushes to create shade; • having curtains and blinds that reduce window space when in open position; • reduction in use of artificial light sources or decreasing wattage of bulbs; • use of lampshades and light fittings that block or absorb large quantities of light emitted.
INCREASE YIN	None	Light is basically yang in nature. Some colours have yin effects but these are dealt with under the section on colour.
DECREASE YIN	None	As above

amount of background information is provided below, however, you should remember that colour is still only one aspect of energy enhancement. If the Feng Shui colour solutions recommended do not particularly appeal to your aesthetic sense, you can look at adjusting the energy of the remainder of the eight energy conditions.

Colour can be applied on a simple or a sophisticated level (where it represents the particular energy needs and colour preferences of an individual). To accommodate these two different approaches, more detailed information has been included (see Note 17 in chapter 5).

Colour vocabulary

To understand colour, and to talk effectively with colour consultants (when selecting paints and fabrics), there are a few words you will need to understand:

- Hue — red, yellow, green and blue are the unitary hues. Hues can also include mixtures of primary colours. Hues are sometimes referred to as tones.
- Tint — a hue mixed with white.
- Shade — a hue mixed with black.

Table 3 — Eliminating excess chi, deficient chi and stagnant chi conditions associated with colour

ENERGY PROBLEM	ENERGY SOLUTION (ENHANCEMENT)	COMMENTS
EXCESS CHI	• Reduce use of bright, harsh colours, particularly reds. • Reduce the numbers of colours used, particularly where they are conflicting.	This can be done by either changing the colour or by using a more subdued tint or hue.
DEFICIENT CHI	• Increase use of bright colours, particularly reds.	This can be done by either changing the colour or by using a brighter tint or hue.
STAGNANT CHI	• Reduce any use of yellowy greens, and lighten colours generally.	

Table 4 — Using colour in accordance with personal energy objectives

ENERGY OBJECTIVE	ENERGY ENHANCEMENT	COMMENTS
INCREASE YANG	• Increase use of red, orange and gold. • Make colours brighter generally. • Increase colour contrasts.	This can be done by using a brighter tint or hue.
DECREASE YANG	• Decrease use of red, orange and gold. • Make colours more subdued. • Decrease colour contrasts.	This can be done by using a duller tint or hue.
INCREASE YIN	• Increase use of blue, black and green. • Make colours more subdued.	This can be done by using a duller tint or hue.
DECREASE YIN	• Decrease use of blue, black and green. • Make colours brighter.	This can be done by using a brighter tint or hue.

- Saturation — the intensity of colour from pale to dark.
- Lightness — how close a colour is to white or black.
- Temperature — whether the colour appears to have a hot or cold feel.
- Movement — whether the colour appears to be advancing or retreating. The most luminous colours advance, the least luminous retreat. Red is a stationary colour.

To keep different colours used in the one room equal 'strength', remember that the less you use of one colour the deeper it should be.

Identifying excess, deficient and stagnant chi conditions
When considering colour, excess chi refers to environments which are either excessively bright or have too many colours in them; deficient chi means the environment has colours that are too pale and bleak, or that there is insufficient variation in colour. Some colours are also regarded as 'stagnant', such as yellowy greens, olives and puce.

Electromagnetic radiation and fields
Background
Electromagnetic fields have always been found in our environment. Both the planet and our bodies naturally possess such fields. However, modern technology has significantly increased the strength and number of electromagnetic fields encountered. Because of the excess chi nature of many electromagnetic fields associated with this technology, it is better to focus on reducing exposure to artificial electromagnetic fields, regardless of personal energy objectives.

EARTH'S MAGNETIC FIELD

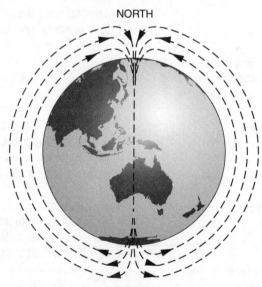

The direction of all the arrows is north. Our feeling that north is always in one 'direction' is an error arising from the fact that the world is a sphere, rather than flat as we perceive it.

Table 5 — Eliminating excess chi, deficient chi and stagnant chi conditions associated with electromagnetic fields

ENERGY PROBLEM	ENERGY SOLUTION (ENHANCEMENT)	COMMENTS
EXCESS CHI	• Buy 'shielded', low-emission electrical equipment.	This is particularly important for TV screens, computers and any equipment to which you stay close (within 1 metre) for extended periods of time. With computer or TV screens, be particularly careful not to spend extended periods of time in an area up to 1 metre behind the unit.
	• Avoid having active electrical fields within 1 metre of your body while sleeping.	Consider digital clocks, electric blankets. Don't forget to consider what lies on the other side of the wall against which your bedhead rests. You need only be concerned about equipment that is actually running while you sleep. With external walls the proximity of your fuse box may have to be considered.
	• Microwave emissions should be avoided where possible.	
DEFICIENT CHI	None	Deficient chi is not really a problem with electromagnetic fields, since we cannot avoid being within the earth's geomagnetic field.
STAGNANT CHI	None	Very low-frequency fields could be regarded as stagnant chi but you are not likely to encounter these outside of industrialised areas.

This does not mean you have to get rid of all electrical equipment. The costs in terms of lifestyle would outweigh the benefits obtained. It makes sense, however, to reduce exposure to artificially created electromagnetic fields as much as you can.

Table 6 — Adjusting electromagnetic field energy in accordance with personal energy objectives

ENERGY OBJECTIVE	ENERGY ENHANCEMENT	COMMENTS
INCREASE YANG	None	It is not recommended to increase yang energy with artificial electromagnetic fields, as these are generally excess chi in nature.
DECREASE YANG	• Reduce number of electrical appliances. • Keep electrical appliances off when not in use. • When purchasing electrical equipment, particularly computers, check to see if the electromagnetic radiation emitted is classified as 'low'.	
INCREASE YIN	None	Electrical fields are yang in nature.
DECREASE YIN	None	Electrical fields are yang in nature.

There may still be valid reasons to seek to increase the electromagnetic fields that you are exposed to (as in magnetic healing). However, the area is a specialised one and I do not recommend that you attempt to adjust the chi of your environment by deliberately increasing the strength and number of electromagnetic fields present in it.

General notes
• If you live very close to high transmission lines, substations or other electrical installations, it would be sensible to measure the electric fields to which you are being subjected, to make sure that they fall within recommended limits.
• There are some indications that children may be more susceptible than adults to the effect of electric fields.

Mirrors

Background

The two most common energy-enhancing tools found in Feng Shui are mirrors and crystals. Indeed, because of their versatility in effecting cures, mirrors are sometimes called the 'aspirin' of Feng Shui (see Note 15 and Note 18 in chapter 5).

Identifying excess, deficient and stagnant chi conditions

Mirrors can cause excess chi by moving light energy around too fast. They can help cure deficient chi and stagnant chi situations but, because of the yang nature of light, cannot create these conditions.

Table 7 — Eliminating excess chi, deficient chi and stagnant chi conditions associated with mirrors

ENERGY PROBLEM	ENERGY SOLUTION (ENHANCEMENT)	COMMENTS
EXCESS CHI	• Generally reduce size and number of mirrors. • Use mirrors to reflect away excess chi entering property or dwelling.	This reduces circulation of energy. This reduces quantum of energy. The mirror is placed outside the house or reflects excess chi directly out of the window. The reflection of the external view should not be visible to occupants.
DEFICIENT CHI	• Generally increase size and number of mirrors. • Use mirrors to draw chi into a dwelling.	This increases circulation of energy. This increases quantum of energy. The mirror is generally placed on the back wall of a room or where the reflection of the external view is visible to occupants.
STAGNANT CHI	• Generally increase size and number of mirrors.	This increases circulation of energy.

Controlling light with mirrors
Mirrors can be used to move light, to deflect non-beneficial light energy patterns and bring in beneficial light energy patterns.

Adjusting the internal circulation of chi
Mirrors help to circulate chi.

Symbols
Pictures or photographs, etc., containing images of mirrors can help to stimulate the flow of chi but at a much lower level than is achieved by using an actual mirror or image-reflecting surface.

Crystals
Background
In this section we are interested in the effects that crystals have on light, that is, their ability to disperse it. This is different to reflection because the nature of the crystal is to pass the light through itself, thus bending and splitting the light into many new directions.

This feature of crystals can be used to disperse excess chi by basically reducing the quantity of energy that is travelling in any one direction. Crystals can also be used to ensure that energy reaches

Table 8 — Using mirrors in accordance with personal energy objectives

ENERGY OBJECTIVE	ENERGY ENHANCEMENT	COMMENTS
INCREASE YANG	Increase size and number of mirrors.	Do not create excess chi conditions.
DECREASE YANG	Decrease size and number of mirrors.	Do not create deficient chi or stagnant chi conditions.
INCREASE YIN	Decrease size and number of mirrors.	Do not create deficient chi or stagnant chi conditions.
DECREASE YIN	Increase size and number of mirrors	Do not create excess chi conditions.

111

Table 9 — Eliminating excess chi, deficient chi and stagnant chi conditions associated with crystals

ENERGY PROBLEM	ENERGY SOLUTION (ENHANCEMENT)	COMMENTS
EXCESS CHI	• Use crystals to disperse excess chi.	This does not reduce total quantum of energy but can disperse streams of strong energy.
SI CHI	• Use crystals to overcome deficient chi by dispersing existing energy.	Cutglass crystals can only spread energy about, not increase total energy. They are therefore useful for situations where only a part of a room has a deficient chi condition.
STAGNANT CHI	• Use crystals to overcome deficient chi by dispersing existing energy.	This increases circulation of energy.

Table 10 — Using crystals in accordance with personal energy objectives

ENERGY OBJECTIVE	ENERGY ENHANCEMENT	COMMENTS
INCREASE YANG	Increase size and number of crystals.	Do not create excess chi conditions.
DECREASE YANG	Decrease size and number of crystals.	Do not create deficient chi or stagnant chi conditions.
INCREASE YIN	Decrease size and number of crystals.	Do not create deficient chi or stagnant chi conditions.
DECREASE YIN	Increase size and number of crystals.	Do not create excess chi conditions.

areas of rooms that would otherwise be deficient in chi or contain stagnant chi.

Crystals have other properties apart from the dispersion and reflection of light (see Note 15 in chapter 5).

Visual arts and symbols

Background

One very important aspect of light is the patterns in which it comes. Let's take two pictures, one of a bright spring scene and another one of the aftermath of a battle, depicting slain and injured combatants. The fact that we feel our mood change when our attention shifts from one picture to another is an indication of the powerful energetic effect that can be achieved simply by changing a pattern of light.

Many artworks (and this includes photographs, films, video compilations, and so forth) may be great art in their ability to shock the observer into viewing the world from a new perspective and may

Table 11 — Eliminating excess chi, deficient chi and stagnant chi conditions associated with visual arts

ENERGY PROBLEM	ENERGY SOLUTION (ENHANCEMENT)	COMMENTS
EXCESS CHI	• Remove pictures depicting violent imagery. • Reduce time that televisions and computers depict violent imagery.	Avoid scenes of battles, fighting/killing (including hunting scenes) and natural violence such as storms. Also avoid abstract art with many sharp lines and angles. Heavy waterfalls.
DEFICIENT CHI	• Introduce pictures depicting energetic scenes.	These include scenes with colour and energy — a sunrise, ocean movement, city scenes, boats on water, pastoral scenes.
STAGNANT CHI	• Introduce scenes with movement.	These include waves on rocks, waterfalls, fountains, movement of people.

well rate a central place in an art gallery or its equivalent. However, whether they should be introduced into your home or work environment is another question. What you should be aware of is that patterns of light, from whatever media they are sourced, have powerful energetic effects and whether we use these effects knowingly or unknowingly, they will still be there. This section is a guide as to how you may use such effects for your own advantage.

Tips and advice
The energetic effect depends on the light pattern being visible. Pictures are generally hung on a wall and are visible throughout the day. If you buy a picture to achieve a certain energetic effect and then lock it away

Table 12 — Adjusting visual art energy in accordance with personal energy objectives

ENERGY OBJECTIVE	ENERGY ENHANCEMENT	COMMENTS
INCREASE YANG	• Use visual art that has gold and red colours, depicts movement and activity or otherwise symbolises heat and energy.	Whatever the colours, do not use pictures that depict snow and ice scenes or bodies of still water. Be careful with the use of hot desert pictures as these can represent deficient chi situations. Spring and summer scenes are good.
DECREASE YANG	Reduce visual art that has gold and reds, depicts movement or otherwise symbolises energy.	
INCREASE YIN	Use visual art that has blues and greens, that depicts rest and stillness or otherwise symbolises coldness and tranquillity.	Autumn and winter scenes are good.
DECREASE YIN	Reduce visual art that has gold and reds, depicts movement or otherwise symbolises energy.	

in a cupboard, don't anticipate it will have much effect. Similarly, photographs displayed on walls or in frames will have a more significant effect than those in albums that are only infrequently viewed.

Televisions and computers generally display images for short periods of time, thus, the images may be seen as relatively unimportant. However, constantly replaying images or playing many similar images over a long period of time will have significant energetic effects.

You can utilise technology to adjust energy conditions by having pleasing scenes on your television and computer screen saver.

Symbols
The visual arts are, of course, symbols in themselves.

Sound environment energy enhancement techniques

Background
Remember that sound is simply the way in which we become aware of pressure waves in our environment. The vibration of sound permeates our whole environment and is a significant indicator of the state of its underlying chi.

For practical reasons, this section focuses on audible sound. You should remember, however, that the range of hearing and sensitivity to sound decreases with age. Babies, young children and pets may be sensitive to high-frequency sounds you cannot hear, making their reactions useful guides to the presence of high-frequency sound. Try turning appliances on and off in their presence. If they become disturbed and move away for no apparent reason, then that piece of electrical equipment may be emitting high-frequency sound, which means you may need to move it further away or cover it with some sound-absorbent material (without contravening the manufacturer's instructions regarding ventilation, etc.).

Identifying excess, deficient and stagnant chi conditions
Excess chi conditions are evidenced by a sound environment that:
• is too loud;
• contains unpleasant sounds that cause a physical reaction (think about chalk sounds on a blackboard, scraping metals together); and/or

- contains very high-frequency sounds (think about a dog whistle or the whine of an electric or mechanical motor under stress).

Deficient chi conditions are evidenced by a sound environment that:
- is too quiet; and
- contains very low-frequency sounds.

Stagnant chi conditions are evidenced by a sound environment that contains dull repetitive sounds, such as that of a dripping tap.

Creating a controllable sound environment

When you have just spent the last four hours listening to your neighbour play loud music, you might think that your sound environment is not a very controllable one. There is, however, quite a lot you can do.

Sound can be deflected in the same way as light; the problem is that thin, lightweight materials begin to resonate with the same vibration as the original sound. The more massive and rigid the material the less this will happen.

A sound can also be transformed by mixing it with other unstructured sound such as that created by running water or wind through leaves. It is also possible to mask sounds by playing your own music or natural sounds. However, structured sounds like music cannot be masked with other music — this only creates discordant sound. It would be better to use sounds like that of the sea crashing on the beach.

Internal fountains and motor-driven waterfalls are great ways to modify your sound environment. They are lovely to listen to during the day but can be turned off at night when they might disturb your sleep.

Adjusting the internal circulation of chi

Sound, by its very nature, tends to encourage the circulation of chi. Hanging bells and wind chimes can be a particularly effective way of doing this.

Adjusting the quality of sound chi

If you want to understand quality of chi in sound then think about the human voice. The chi embodied by a harsh, angry voice is a world

Table 13 — Eliminating excess chi, deficient chi and stagnant chi conditions associated with sound

ENERGY PROBLEM	ENERGY SOLUTION (ENHANCEMENT)	COMMENTS
EXCESS CHI	• Lower the sound energy in an environment.	This can be done by deflection (walls, double-glazing), absorption (sound insulation or by increasing fabric in the environment), transformation (mixing with white sound from waterfalls and fountains) or elimination (removing the source of the sound if it is on your property).
	• Identify and mask unpleasant sounds.	Playing music, creating white-sound sources.
DEFICIENT CHI	• Introduce sound.	This includes music, fountains, waterfalls; planting of trees and bushes that create pleasant sounds in the wind or the rain; birds (even if only encouraging them in your garden); aquariums with an aerator.
	• Reduce use of materials that deflect or absorb sound.	Open doors and windows, reduce curtains and fabric, increase use of tiles and ceramics.
STAGNANT CHI	• Use bells and wind chimes, artificial waterfalls and fountains.	These can be the real thing or natural sounds contained on CDs and tapes.

away from that of a voice embodying love and concern — it is not a matter of volume. Even if you do not understand the language, or cannot see the person talking, you will have no difficulty recognising the difference. Of course, a person can disguise their true emotion when speaking but all this means is that we know how to change the inherent nature of the energy we put into the sounds we utter.

Table 14 — Adjusting sound energy in accordance with personal energy objectives

ENERGY OBJECTIVE	ENERGY ENHANCEMENT	COMMENTS
INCREASE YANG	Increase yang sound energy and sound level generally. Reduce sounds that make you sleepy and relaxed.	Yang sounds include waterfalls and fountains, waves on beach or rocks, 'stirring' music, bells and wind chimes.
DECREASE YANG	Decrease yang sound energy and sound generally. Increase sounds that make you sleepy and relaxed.	Yang sounds include waterfalls and fountains, waves on beach or rocks, 'stirring' music, bells and wind chimes.
INCREASE YIN	Increase proportion of yin sound and reduce sound level overall.	Yin sounds include lapping water, rustling trees, soft bird-sound. Relaxing music (such as 'New Age' music) is ideal.
DECREASE YIN	Reduce proportion of yin sound and increase sound level overall.	Yin sounds include lapping water, rustling trees, soft bird-sound. Relaxing music (such as 'New Age' music) is ideal.

Again, without making any inherent aesthetic judgments, we know from experiments that plants seem to be healthier and grow better when exposed to classical music as opposed to rock music. For humans also, some music seems better for healing, reflection and growth, while other types are more stirring. Try staying still when military music is played!

You will have no more problem recognising beneficial music than you will a pleasant voice. The trick is to distinguish between what you enjoy and what is good for you. Most of us recognise that while we may like ice-cream and chocolate, large amounts of these do not make a sound foundation for a good diet.

Symbols
One obvious symbol of sound is a musical instrument. Naturally, the sound symbolised by a drum is quite different to that of a flute or any other melodic and harmonious-sounding instrument and will have a more yang effect on the energy of the environment.

Pictures of music being played can also evoke sound. Again, there would be a difference between a picture or poster of a heavy-metal rock group and one of a classical orchestra. Pictures and ornaments representing birds may also evoke sound, although such a representation is not particularly powerful as a sound symbol.

Movement energy environment enhancement techniques

Background
Moving objects — people, animals, fish, air, water and mechanical devices — are a necessary part of any environment that has beneficial, or sheng, chi.

Identifying excess, deficient and stagnant chi conditions
Excess chi movement conditions exist in, for example, busy main roads or other places where there is much movement of people or mechanical objects. You will tend to find excess chi situations exist when large numbers of people leave theatres and sporting events, or when large numbers of shoppers attend sales. Excess chi situations can also exist naturally and are associated with windstorms, torrential rain, floodwaters, avalanches and blizzards.

Deficient chi situations exist where there is little or no movement. This is experienced naturally with, for instance, temperature inversions, which trap the air below in unmoving pockets. Deficient chi situations can be created by having poor ventilation or a still, lifeless environment.

With moving energy, stagnant chi is almost always involved where there has been little or no movement for some time.

Creating a controllable 'movement' environment

A lot of movement energy comes to us from outside our dwelling or property. Blinds and curtains can be used to shut out or draw attention to this moving energy. Wind chimes or vegetation that rustles in the breeze draw attention to moving energy and enhance its effects. Windmills, fountains, artificial waterfalls and mobiles can all be used to create moving energy.

Adjusting the circulation of chi

Movement energy, by its very nature, involves the circulation of chi and the faster moving the components of the environment are, the more chi will be circulated.

Table 15 — Eliminating excess chi, deficient chi and stagnant chi conditions associated with moving energy

ENERGY PROBLEM	ENERGY SOLUTION (ENHANCEMENT)	COMMENTS
EXCESS CHI	• Place barriers between your dwelling and excessive movement of people, vehicles or wind.	This can be as simple as closing the curtains or it could involve building a boundary wall or growing a vegetation screen or windbreak.
DEFICIENT CHI	• Introduce movement into your environment.	This includes: windmills, fountains, waterfalls, bird life, pets and aquariums, pictures of moving things; and ornaments and decorations representing moving things.
STAGNANT CHI	• Introduce movement into your environment.	This includes: windmills, fountains, waterfalls, bird life, pets, aquariums, pictures of moving things and ornaments and decorations representing moving things.

Adjusting the quality of moving chi

Moving chi has quality as well as quantity. Flowing and harmonious movements are far more beneficial than are jerky, irregular ones. Note how you feel when you watch the smooth, flowing movements of arts such as Tai Chi; or the movement of pine or willow trees in gentle winds (the Chinese often talk of 'pine waves' or 'willow waves' to express the movement of these trees). You might also think of seaweed moving under the current of waves. When many objects move in coordination, it tends to be beneficial.

Table 16 — Adjusting moving energy in accordance with personal energy objectives

ENERGY OBJECTIVE	ENERGY ENHANCEMENT	COMMENTS
INCREASE YANG	Generally increase amount and speed of movement in the environment.	Add fountains, waterfalls, birds, fans and windmills. Increase views of moving energy and exposures to breezes.
DECREASE YANG	Generally decrease amount and speed of movement in the environment.	This will often involve screening off views of moving energy outside the property and generally slowing down the movement of air (while maintaining good ventilation).
INCREASE YIN	Generally decrease amount and speed of movement in the environment.	This will often involve screening off views of moving energy outside the property and generally slowing down the movement of air (while maintaining good ventilation).
DECREASE YIN	Generally increase amount and speed of movement in the environment.	Add fountains, waterfalls, birds, fans, and windmills. Increase views of moving energy and exposure to breezes.

The movement of a gently flowing river or stream is more beneficial than that of a thundering waterfall or rapid.

Symbols
Pictures and ornaments depicting any sort of windmill can symbolise movement, as can those of flying birds, swimming fish and other moving animals, pictures of busy scenes, trains, cars and other moving vehicles. Pictures of car/horse races, running races, etc., can be used, but with a little more caution, as these may suggest or symbolise excess chi.

Crystallised energy environment enhancement techniques

Background
Crystallised energy is the energetic impact of the physical objects in your environment. Physical objects involve static patterns of energy, which makes them easy to select and use in order to achieve specific energy goals. They are particularly useful when working to strengthen the eight major life energies.

Identifying excess, deficient and stagnant chi conditions
Excess chi situations are rare with physical objects in your environment. They might be associated with the presence of radioactive material, strong poisons (those which have contaminated the environment rather than those sealed up in bottles and containers) or a very excessive amount of crystals.

Deficient chi situations exist where the physical objects cannot maintain their physical integrity and are near or at the point of failure, resulting from poor design, ageing or wear and tear.

Stagnant chi conditions exist where physical objects are in a state of decomposition, that is, decaying food, compost heaps, areas with mould and fungus, and rotting wood and buildings suffering from concrete cancer.

Creating a controlled crystallised energy environment
As indicated above, working with your physical environment is an ideal way to enhance energy in the eight major life conditions. I

have therefore provided one table for each of these, showing the various physical remedies for each. You can also refer to Note 7 (in chapter 5) about *ba gua* diagrams for determining the most effective places to position these physical objects in your dwelling, garden or workplace.

Another specialised technique for enhancing various life energies is the creation of a fortune table (see Note 14 in chapter 5).

Adjusting the internal circulation of chi
Physical objects or crystallised energy are not useful in controlling the circulation of energy.

Adjusting the quality of crystallised energy
Mineral crystals (as opposed to cutglass crystals) can be used to enhance the quality of chi in very specific ways (see Note 15 in chapter 5).

Some people are concerned about the quality of energy that might be contained within second-hand items. This is not of particular concern (refer to Chapter 1).

Symbols
Most of the enhancements in this area are of a symbolic nature and suggestions as to the specific symbols to use for each of the eight major life energies are detailed on the following tables.

Table 17 — Eliminating excess chi, deficient chi and stagnant chi conditions associated with crystallised energy

ENERGY PROBLEM	ENERGY SOLUTION (ENHANCEMENT)	COMMENTS
EXCESS CHI	• Remove physical objects causing excess chi from environment.	These are objects such as poisons and other elements that, by their very nature, have adverse effects on human beings.
DEFICIENT CHI	• Remove or repair items that are near or at the point of failure or breakdown.	Structural failure of building or mechanical components can be very important.
STAGNANT CHI	• Remove or isolate items that are in the process of decomposition, decay or putrification.	Household garbage and garden waste are usually the main elements here.

Table 18 — Enhancing crystallised energy in accordance with personal energy objectives for career or mission in life

ENERGY OBJECTIVE	ENERGY ENHANCEMENT	COMMENTS
INCREASE YANG	Add pictures, photographs or memorabilia that symbolise your mission or career in life. These objects should symbolise the activities that you carry out in your career or mission — the goals that you wish to achieve.	For greatest effect, place in the career area of dwelling, room or workplace (see Note 8 in chapter 5).

ENERGY OBJECTIVE	ENERGY ENHANCEMENT	COMMENTS
DECREASE YANG	Reduce the number of pictures, photographs or memorabilia that symbolise your mission or career in life. These objects should symbolise the activities that you carry out in your career or mission — the goals that you wish to achieve.	Moving such objects out of the career area of your dwelling, room or workplace will also decrease their energetic impact. You may want to decrease yang when this life energy is dominating your life to the detriment of other aspects or where there is much activity and effort but little achieved.
INCREASE YIN	Add pictures, photographs or memorabilia that symbolise your mission or career in life. These objects should symbolise the things that are important to success in your career or mission — your qualifications, the knowledge or resources you need.	For greatest effect, place in the career area of dwelling, room or workplace (see Note 8 in chapter 5).
DECREASE YIN	Reduce the number of pictures, photographs or memorabilia that symbolise your mission or career in life. These objects should symbolise the activities that you carry out in your career or mission — the goals that you wish to achieve.	Moving such objects out of the career area of your dwelling, room or workplace will also decrease their energetic impact. You may want to decrease yin when this life energy is not as significant a part of life as you would like it to be or where the preparation and building done to support your career or mission seems to be slowing down any actual accomplishment.

Table 19 — Enhancing crystallised energy in accordance with personal energy objectives for inner wisdom and knowledge

ENERGY OBJECTIVE	ENERGY ENHANCEMENT	COMMENTS
INCREASE YANG	Add pictures, photographs or memorabilia that symbolise your knowledge and wisdom. These objects should symbolise the application of this wisdom and knowledge rather than its acquisition.	For greatest effect, place in the knowledge and inner wisdom area of dwelling, room or workplace (see Note 8 in chapter 5).
DECREASE YANG	Reduce the number of pictures, photographs or memorabilia that symbolise your knowledge and wisdom. These objects should symbolise the application of this wisdom and knowledge rather than its acquisition.	Moving such objects out of the knowledge and inner wisdom area of your dwelling, room or workplace will also decrease their energetic impact. You may want to decrease yang when this life energy is dominating your life to the detriment of other aspects or where there is much activity and effort but with little achieved.
INCREASE YIN	Increase the number of pictures, photographs or memorabilia that symbolise your knowledge and wisdom. These objects should symbolise the acquisition of this wisdom and knowledge rather than its use or application.	For greatest effect, place in the knowledge and inner wisdom area of dwelling, room or workplace (see Note 8 in chapter 5).

ENERGY OBJECTIVE	ENERGY ENHANCEMENT	COMMENTS
DECREASE YIN	Decrease the number of pictures, photographs or memorabilia that symbolise your knowledge and wisdom. These objects should symbolise the acquisition of this wisdom and knowledge rather than its use or application.	Moving such objects out of the knowledge and inner wisdom areas of your dwelling, room or workplace will also decrease their energetic impact. You may want to decrease yin when this life energy is not as significant a part of life as you would like it to be or where the preparation and building done to support your career or mission seems to be slowing down any actual accomplishment.

Table 20 — Enhancing crystallised energy in accordance with personal energy objectives for family and health

ENERGY OBJECTIVE	ENERGY ENHANCEMENT	COMMENTS
INCREASE YANG	Increase the number of pictures, photographs or memorabilia that symbolise your family and the health of its members. These objects should symbolise the family, or healthy, activities that you carry out or wish to carry out.	For greatest effect, place in the family and health area of dwelling, room or workplace (see Note 8 in chapter 5).

ENERGY OBJECTIVE	ENERGY ENHANCEMENT	COMMENTS
DECREASE YANG	Reduce the number of pictures, photographs or memorabilia that symbolise your family and the health of its members. These objects should symbolise the family, or healthy, activities that you carry out or wish to carry out.	Moving such objects out of the family and health area of your dwelling, room or workplace will also decrease their energetic impact. You may want to decrease yang when this life energy is dominating your life to the detriment of other aspects or where there is much activity and effort but with little achieved.
INCREASE YIN	Increase the number of pictures, photographs or memorabilia that symbolise your family and the health of its members. These objects should symbolise the things you have done to make your family or health strong.	For greatest effect, place in the family and health area of dwelling, room or workplace (see Note 8 in chapter 5).
DECREASE YIN	Reduce the number of pictures, photographs or memorabilia that symbolise your family and the health of its members. These objects should symbolise the things you have done to make your family or health strong.	Moving such objects out of the family and health area of your dwelling, room or workplace will also decrease their energetic impact. You may want to decrease yin when this life energy is not as significant a part of life as you would like it to be or where the preparation and building done to support your career or mission seems to be slowing down any actual accomplishment.

Table 21 — Enhancing crystallised energy in accordance with personal energy objectives for wealth and prosperity

ENERGY OBJECTIVE	ENERGY ENHANCEMENT	COMMENTS
INCREASE YANG	Increase the number of pictures, photographs or memorabilia that symbolise your wealth and prosperity. These objects should symbolise the lifestyle you wish to lead.	For greatest effect, place in the wealth and prosperity area of dwelling, room or workplace (see Note 8 in chapter 5).
DECREASE YANG	Reduce the number of pictures, photographs or memorabilia that symbolise your wealth and prosperity. These objects should symbolise the lifestyle you wish to lead.	Moving such objects out of the wealth and prosperity areas of your dwelling, room or workplace will also decrease their energetic impact. You may want to decrease yang when this life energy is dominating your life to the detriment of other aspects or where there is much activity and effort but with little achieved.
INCREASE YIN	Increase the number of pictures, photographs or memorabilia that symbolise your wealth and prosperity. These objects should symbolise the things that you see as the source of your wealth and prosperity — your business or career, investments, bank account, money, gold and other precious metals, and money symbols.	For greatest effect, place in the wealth and prosperity area of dwelling, room or workplace (see Note 8 in chapter 5).

ENERGY OBJECTIVE	ENERGY ENHANCEMENT	COMMENTS
DECREASE YIN	Decrease the number of pictures, photographs or memorabilia that symbolise your wealth and prosperity. These objects should symbolise the things that you see as the source of your wealth and prosperity — your business or career, investments, bank account, money, gold and other precious metals, and money symbols.	Moving such objects out of the wealth and prosperity area of your dwelling, room or workplace will also decrease their energetic impact. You may want to decrease yin when this life energy is not as significant a part of life as you would like it to be or where the preparation and building done to support your career or mission seems to be slowing down any actual accomplishment.

Table 22 — Enhancing crystallised energy in accordance with personal energy objectives for reputation and fame

ENERGY OBJECTIVE	ENERGY ENHANCEMENT	COMMENTS
INCREASE YANG	Increase the number of pictures, photographs or memorabilia that symbolise fame and reputation. These objects should symbolise the fame and reputation you would like to have.	For greatest effect, place in the fame and reputation area of dwelling, room or workplace (see Note 8 in chapter 5).

ENERGY OBJECTIVE	ENERGY ENHANCEMENT	COMMENTS
DECREASE YANG	Increase the number of pictures, photographs or memorabilia that symbolise fame and reputation. These objects should symbolise the fame and reputation you would like to have.	Moving such objects out of the fame and reputation areas of your dwelling, room or workplace will also decrease their energetic impact. You may want to decrease yang when this life energy is dominating your life to the detriment of other aspects — your privacy may be invaded or people may expect more than you are able to deliver.
INCREASE YIN	Increase the number of pictures, photographs or memorabilia that symbolise fame and reputation. These objects should symbolise the things you have done that should result in fame and reputation.	For greatest effect, place in the fame and reputation area of dwelling, room or workplace (see Note 8 in chapter 5).
DECREASE YIN	Reduce the number of pictures, photographs or memorabilia that symbolise fame and reputation. These objects should symbolise the things you have done that should result in fame and reputation.	Moving such objects out of the reputation and fame area of your dwelling, room or workplace will also decrease their energetic impact. You may want to decrease yin when this life energy is not as significant a part of life as you would like it to be or where your efforts are unrecognised and where people have lower expectations of and trust in you than is deserved.

Table 23 — Enhancing crystallised energy in accordance with personal energy objectives for relationships

ENERGY OBJECTIVE	ENERGY ENHANCEMENT	COMMENTS
INCREASE YANG	Increase the number of pictures, photographs or memorabilia that symbolise your relationships. These objects should symbolise the relationships or aspects of those relationships you would like to achieve.	For greatest effect, place in the relationship area of dwelling, room or workplace (see Note 8 in chapter 5).
DECREASE YANG	Reduce the number of pictures, photographs or memorabilia that symbolise your relationships. These objects should symbolise the relationships or aspects of those relationships you would like to achieve.	Moving such objects out of the relationship area of your dwelling, room or workplace will also decrease their energetic impact. You may want to decrease yang when this life energy is dominating your life to the detriment of other aspects — there may be too many relationships or they may be very volatile.
INCREASE YIN	Increase the number of pictures, photographs or memorabilia that symbolise your relationships. These objects should symbolise the achievements of the relationship — anniversaries, children, dinners, outings and happy events.	For greatest effect place in the relationship area of dwelling, room or workplace (see Note 8 in chapter 5).

ENERGY OBJECTIVE	ENERGY ENHANCEMENT	COMMENTS
DECREASE YIN	Reduce the number of pictures, photographs or memorabilia that symbolise your relationships. These objects should symbolise the achievements of the relationship — anniversaries, children, dinners, outings and happy events.	Moving such objects out of the relationship area of your dwelling, room or workplace will also decrease their energetic impact. You may want to decrease yin when the history of the relationship seems more important than its future, when there is a need for change and growth in the relationship.

Table 24 — Enhancing crystallised energy in accordance with personal energy objectives for creativity and children

ENERGY OJECTIVE	ENERGY ENHANCEMENT	COMMENTS
INCREASE YANG	Increase the number of pictures, photographs or memorabilia that symbolise your creativity and children. These objects should symbolise the things you wish to create or the level of creativity to which you wish to aspire.	For greatest effect, place in the creativity/children area of dwelling, room or workplace (see Note 8 in chapter 5).

ENERGY OJECTIVE	ENERGY ENHANCEMENT	COMMENTS
DECREASE YANG	Reduce the number of pictures, photographs or memorabilia that symbolise your creativity and children. These objects should symbolise the things you wish to create or the level of creativity to which you wish to aspire.	Moving such objects out of the creativity/children area of your dwelling, room or workplace will also decrease their energetic impact. You may want to decrease yang when this life energy is dominating your life to the detriment of other aspects — where there are too many creative projects on the boil with too little actual achievement.
INCREASE YIN	Increase the number of pictures, photographs or memorabilia that symbolise your creativity and children. These objects should symbolise the things you have achieved and the things that set the foundation of future creative acts. In the case of future children this may be your existing relationship.	For greatest effect, place in the creative/children area of dwelling, room or workplace (see Note 8 in chapter 5).
DECREASE YIN	Decrease the number of pictures, photographs or memorabilia that symbolise your creativity and children. These objects should symbolise the things you have achieved and the things that set the foundation of future creative acts.	Moving such objects out of the creativity/children area of your dwelling, room or workplace will also decrease their energetic impact. You may want to decrease yin when this life energy is not as significant a part of life as you would like it to be or where the preparation and building done to support your career or mission seems to be slowing down any actual accomplishment.

Table 25 — Enhancing crystallised energy in accordance with personal energy objectives for helpful people and environments

ENERGY OBJECTIVE	ENERGY ENHANCEMENT	COMMENTS
INCREASE YANG	Increase the number of pictures, photographs or memorabilia that symbolise what you could do with the proper help and support. Where you have a particular travel objective you can add pictures, photographs or ornaments that show or symbolise this destination.	For greatest effect, place in the help and support area of dwelling, room or workplace (see Note 8 in chapter 5).
DECREASE YANG	Reduce the number of pictures, photographs or memorabilia that symbolise what you could do with the proper help and support.	Moving such objects out of the help and support areas of your dwelling, room or workplace will also decrease their energetic impact. You may want to decrease yang when this life energy is dominating your life to the detriment of other aspects or where there is much activity and effort but with little achieved.
INCREASE YIN	Increase the number of pictures photographs or memorabilia that symbolise the type of support and help you would like to have. Where you have a travel objective, you can add pictures, photographs or ornaments that show or symbolise previous travels.	For greatest effect, place in the help and support area of dwelling, room or workplace (see Note 8 in chapter 5).

ENERGY OBJECTIVE	ENERGY ENHANCEMENT	COMMENTS
DECREASE YIN	Reduce the number of pictures, photographs or memorabilia that symbolise the type of support and help you would like to have. Where you have travelled, you can reduce the number of pictures, photographs or ornaments that show or symbolise these travels.	Moving such objects out of the help and support area of your dwelling, room or workplace will also decrease their energetic impact. You may want to decrease yin when this life energy is not as significant a part of life as you would like it to be or where the preparation and building done to support your career or mission seems to be slowing down any actual accomplishment.

Thermal energy environment enhancement techniques

Background

Most of us would be quite familiar with attempting to maintain a healthy thermal environment, although this is generally from the point of view of being comfortable rather than the consideration of energy consequences. Without implying that you freeze or fry in your pursuit of good Feng Shui (which would, anyway, represent deficient or excess chi conditions!), you need to remember that comfort relates to the temperature of the body rather than the temperature of the room. This can be substantially controlled by the clothing worn, leaving you more flexibility in adjusting the temperature of your overall environment.

Remember that the condition of thermal environments may vary with the seasons.

Identifying excess, deficient and stagnant chi conditions

It is simple to work out that excess chi occurs when our environment is too hot and deficient chi occurs when it is too cold. Stagnation of chi tends to occur when temperature is uniform over a number of days.

136

Creating a controlled thermal environment

Heaters, coolers, fans, airconditioners, blinds and fires are all included in our armoury for controlling our thermal environment.

Adjusting the internal circulation of chi

Often we try to cool ourselves down when all we really need to do is circulate the air in order to take away the heat generated by our bodies. Similarly, in cold conditions, reducing the flow of air over your skin (by wearing appropriate clothing) and stopping any draughts may be all that is required.

Adjusting the quality of chi

Try to use as much of the heating effect of the sun as you can.

Symbols

Pictures are one of the best ways to symbolise thermal energy. Pictures of snow-capped mountains and other scenes of ice and snow can capture the yin aspect of thermal energy; pictures of deserts and sunny beaches can symbolise heat, as can those of roaring log fires with families gathered around them.

Table 26 — Eliminating excess chi, deficient chi and stagnant chi conditions associated with thermal energy

ENERGY PROBLEM	ENERGY SOLUTION (ENHANCEMENT)	COMMENTS
EXCESS CHI	• Reduce heat sources.	Minimise use of electrical equipment that can generate considerable heat as by-product.
	• Increase circulation of air.	Use fans.
	• Vary insulation.	Reduce in cold external environments, increase in warm external environments. Natural insulation could be the shade of trees.

ENERGY PROBLEM	ENERGY SOLUTION (ENHANCEMENT)	COMMENTS
	• Use cooling devices.	These include airconditioners, increased ventilation when external environment is cooler.
DEFICIENT CHI	• Increase heat sources.	Use fires and other heating devices.
	• Decrease circulation of air.	Prevent draughts by keeping windows and doors closed. Trees around property can reduce wind-chill factor.
	• Vary insulation.	Increase in cold external environments, decrease in warm external environments. Natural insulation could be the shade of trees.
STAGNANT CHI	• Use fans and ventilation.	

Table 27 — Adjusting thermal energy in accordance with personal energy objectives

ENERGY OBJECTIVE	ENERGY ENHANCEMENT	COMMENTS
INCREASE YANG	Increase heating elements.	Where the external environment is warmer than the internal environment: • increase ventilation; • open blinds, curtains and windows; and/or • reduce shading effect of trees and plants. Where the external environment is cooler than the internal environment, use heating devices.

ENERGY OBJECTIVE	ENERGY ENHANCEMENT	COMMENTS
DECREASE YANG	Decrease heating elements.	Where the external environment is warmer than the internal environment: • decrease ventilation; • close blinds, curtains and windows; and/or • increase shading effect of trees and plants. Where the external environment is cooler than the internal environment, lower the temperature settings of heating devices.
INCREASE YIN	Increase cooling elements.	Where the external environment is warmer than the internal environment, use cooling devices, fans, air coolers and airconditioners. Where the external environment is cooler than the internal environment: • increase ventilation; • open blinds, curtains and windows; and/or • reduce shading effect of trees and plants.

ENERGY OBJECTIVE	ENERGY ENHANCEMENT	COMMENTS
DECREASE YIN	Decrease cooling elements.	Where the external environment is warmer than the internal environment, lower settings on cooling devices, fans, air coolers and airconditioners. Where the external environment is cooler than the internal environment: • increase ventilation; • open blinds, curtains and windows; and • reduce shading effect of trees and plants.

Moisture environment energy enhancement techniques

Background

Water energy can be a very powerful tool for modifying the nature of chi in an environment. You only have to think of how different a garden can be when it has the right supply of water, compared to how it appears when it has had too much or too little.

Identifying excess, deficient and stagnant chi conditions

Excess chi conditions are generally associated with water that is flowing so fast it is tearing away the environment through which it is passing. We think of floods and rivers in spate as culprits, but we should also include large waterfalls which, however beautiful, also create excess chi conditions. In general, excess chi situations and what to do about them are obvious enough at the time. From a Feng Shui management point of view, we need to prevent rather than cure these situations. Plumbing and guttering should be well maintained; natural watercourses (even if usually dry) should be reviewed to see what consequences their flooding would have. Appropriate rectification work can then be done.

Deficient chi conditions are represented by an arid environment.

Stagnant water provides one of the clearest examples of stagnant chi in a moisture environment.

Creating a controlled moisture environment

The level of moisture around us is constantly changing; it would be very convenient if we had a material which released moisture in dry conditions and absorbed moisture in wet conditions. In fact, wood has this very property and when used in an environment can help to balance moisture levels.

Adjusting the internal circulation of chi

Running water, as in fountains, springs, streams, rivers and waterfalls, can help with the movement of chi.

Adjusting the quality of chi

Water should be kept fresh and pure, but there is nothing wrong with water which is teeming with life, as with that in aquariums and garden ponds. The fresher the water in the environment, the better the underlying quality of chi.

Symbols

There are many symbols we can use for water. Pictures of oceans, lakes, rivers and streams are perhaps the most obvious but you should not overlook pictures of rain, mist, clouds, waterfalls, garden ponds, fish and fountains; items made of glass and clear crystal; and rounded river pebbles. Any arrangement of rocks, gravel and sand that creates the illusion of flowing water can also be used. These symbols show water in many guises and can therefore be used to enhance the energetic conditions in either a yin or yang direction.

Table 28 — Eliminating excess chi, deficient chi and stagnant chi conditions associated with moisture energy

ENERGY PROBLEM	ENERGY SOLUTION (ENHANCEMENT)	COMMENTS
EXCESS CHI	• Reduce quantity of water in environment.	In dwellings this generally refers to the moisture content of the air, which then condenses, making surfaces damp.
	• Reduce flow speed of water in environment.	Preventative precautions are best here (see p. 140 'Identifying excess, deficient and stagnant chi conditions').
DEFICIENT CHI	• Introduce water.	In gardens: introduce pools, fountains, waterfalls; increase watering of the garden; and grow trees that create their own moist microclimate. Most of the above solutions can also be carried out, on a lesser scale, within the dwelling.
STAGNANT CHI	• Increase movement of water.	In gardens, get rid of any obvious pools of stagnant water but also try to eliminate perpetually boggy and dank areas by creating drainage or reducing shade. For internal dampness, increase ventilation and light.

Table 29 — Adjusting moisture energy in accordance with personal energy objectives

ENERGY OBJECTIVE	ENERGY ENHANCEMENT	COMMENTS
INCREASE YANG	Increase movement of existing water.	Caution should always be taken when trying to increase yang by introducing more water into an environment as water is, by its nature, yin. It is only really appropriate to do this in deficient chi conditions. However, putting a fountain in an existing point, raising the height of parts of a stream to create waterfalls, increasing the flow of a stream in a manner which increases the sound and movement of a stream are all options. Introducing a small volume of water that is circulated quickly, as in an internal fountain, can be beneficial. Aquariums filled with plants and the movement of fish are good but a lone fish in a non-aerated, plantless aquarium is not.
DECREASE YANG	Make existing water movement in the environment slower and more tranquil.	Caution must be exercised not to create stagnant chi.
INCREASE YIN	Increase volume of water in environment.	Reflection pools, cold-water aquariums or internal fountains where water flows downwards.

ENERGY OBJECTIVE	ENERGY ENHANCEMENT	COMMENTS
DECREASE YIN	Reduce volume of water in an environment.	Outside environments: create drier areas with more desert-like plants such as palms and cacti (they are not all spiny!). Internal environments: increase ventilation and decrease quantity of plant life.

Bio-energy environment enhancement techniques

Background
Appropriate bio-energy can help to create sheng (beneficial) chi within an environment. Bio-energy is sourced from any living things, be they plant, animal, fish, insect, bird or reptile. These can be pets or wildlife.

Identifying excess, deficient and stagnant chi conditions
Excess chi is created when there is simply too much bio-energy on the premises, resulting from either too many animals or plants, or the energy from any of these simply being too strong. A dozen dogs or cats in a city flat would create excess chi, while the same number on a large country farm might be quite appropriate. Due to their nature, a tiger in the house, crocodile in the back garden or shark in the swimming pool would be likely to create excess chi. Even a flock of cockatoos on your property can create excess chi! In general, an excess of plant, and in particular, insect life, will tend to create stagnant chi rather than excess chi conditions, the exception being spiky or thorned plants which can, if dominant in an environment, create sha chi.

Deficient chi reflects a sterile, inorganic environment such as one you might associate with a hospital or food-processing area. There are certainly benefits to be obtained from these but they do not make good living environments.

Stagnant chi is usually associated with infestation, when populations grow out of control. Rats, cockroaches, flies, maggots, algal blooms and fungi are all representative of stagnant chi conditions.

Creating a controlled bio-energy environment

It is relatively easy to adjust the amount of plant life in a house and garden, and we can acquire and discard plants at will. The situation with animals is a little different (disposing of the cat or dog because it did not fit your energy plans would require a rather callous nature!). Always think carefully about the energetic impact that any animal you propose to introduce into an environment is going to have. If that impact isn't suitable for you, the environment is unlikely to be suitable for the animal.

Adjusting the internal circulation of chi

In general terms, animal life will tend to speed up the circulation of chi while plants will tend to slow it down. There is one thing to note here. During the daytime, plants convert the energy of light into various chemical compounds (applied towards growth) — which is basically a yin process. During the night, this process of photosynthesis stops and the only remaining one is the ongoing metabolism and growth of the plant — a yang process. Humans are the reverse, being more yin during the night and more yang in the day, which means it is not a good idea to have lots of plants in the bedroom. You must also consider that plants have both colour and aroma; if you are keeping plants in the bedroom, they should not be brightly coloured or strong-smelling, as these energies may disturb sleep. If you must keep plants in the bedroom, try to use leafy green plants with soft, round leaves.

Adjusting the quality of chi

As I have previously indicated when one has a pet that one can bond with there are Feng Shui benefits. It is important to differentiate between a 'bond' and a fascination or admiration for an animal's ferocity or the danger it represents. If one keeps a ferocious dog (or any animal) that one has to dominate constantly or protect oneself from, the Feng Shui aspects are negative. Animals, then, can have a variety of positive and negative effects on the quality of Chi.

Symbols

If you cannot have the real thing then it may be appropriate to use symbols of plants and animals. Such symbols may be found in pictures and ornaments. Also, these symbols may be used on curtains, fabrics, carpets and wallpaper. Sometimes animal and plants symbols are incorporated into leadlighting and transparencies, which can be attached to windows.

Children in particular often have lots of animal symbols in their bedroom. During the day, pictures of leaping lions and tigers, a bedspread depicting zoo animals and a bed filled with stuffed toy animals may match the exuberant energy of the child. During the night, however, all this symbolic bio-energy can have a disturbing effect on them. If the child's bedroom is filled with symbols of powerful, active and ferocious animals and their behaviour tends to be hyperactive, you should look at removing some of these symbols and replacing them with more passive and relaxing ones.

While symbols, either in the form of ornaments or paintings of tigers and dragons, should be used with caution, they can be advantageous in situations where you need to be a little more assertive or where any aspect of your life is under threat. However, if you are having problems with conflict and aggression, symbols of tigers and lions, and like animals, should be removed.

Table 30 — Eliminating excess chi, deficient chi and stagnant chi conditions associated with bio-energy

ENERGY PROBLEM	ENERGY SOLUTION (ENHANCEMENT)	COMMENTS
EXCESS CHI	• Transfer inappropriate plant or animal to more suitable environment.	There is nothing 'wrong' with any plant or animal but it may simply not belong in your environment (or you in its environment!).
DEFICIENT CHI	• Introduce plants and animals suitable to the environment.	These could be pets, indoor plants, increased vegetation in the garden, plants that attract birds to your garden, fish in aquariums or ponds. Healthy garden ponds will generally attract all sorts of life.

ENERGY PROBLEM	ENERGY SOLUTION (ENHANCEMENT)	COMMENTS
STAGNANT CHI	• Reduce number of plants and increase number of animals.	This applies to both internal and external environments.

Table 31 — Adjusting bio-energy in accordance with personal energy objectives

ENERGY OBJECTIVE	ENERGY ENHANCEMENT	COMMENTS
INCREASE YANG	Increase the number or liveliness of animals within the environment.	While the individual personality of an animal can lead to variations in this, the yang effect, in general, in descending order, is: • diurnal (daytime) animals; • nocturnal animals; • birds; • reptiles; • tropical fish; • cold-water fish. The more active the animal the more yang its effect.
DECREASE YANG	Decrease the number or liveliness aspect of animals within the environment.	
INCREASE YIN	Increase the amount of plants or vegetation.	Plants with yin effects, in descending order, are: • soft, green plants; • plants with rigid trunks and branches; • spiny, spiky, brownish-coloured plants.
DECREASE YIN	Reduce the amount of plants or vegetation, or increase their rigidity.	

Aroma environment energy enhancement techniques

Background

The smell of an environment can be a vital indicator as to the quality of the underlying chi. As a consequence, changing (as opposed to masking) that smell can have significant energetic impacts.

Identifying excess, deficient and stagnant chi conditions

An aroma indicative of excess chi is generally of a burnt, scorched, acrid nature. It also includes sharp, pungent smells (such as the aroma of smelling salts).

In a deficient chi environment the smell will either be faint or have an antiseptic or 'metallic' nature; although, if the smell is strong, it will be more indicative of excess chi.

Stagnant chi is indicated by a rotten, decaying, putrid smell, and also smells of a 'cloying' nature.

All sources of these smells should be eliminated as soon as detected (or, in the case of smelling salts, as soon as they have worked!).

Creating a controlled aroma environment

It is important to understand the difference between masking and actually changing an aroma. If a stronger aroma is used to mask another aroma that is still present, then you will have slightly improved but not significantly changed the underlying chi. Masking would be tantamount to covering up a damp wall with wood panelling — it might look good at first but, sooner or later, the true nature of the environment would permeate through.

If the aroma of your environment is basically good then it is certainly possible to enhance it significantly by introducing appropriate scents. Herbs grown in pots and containers can be useful, as they can be moved in and out of the house as required. The scent of flowers often supports the energy of the season (especially when the plant is native to the area) and, again, some of these can be brought into the house in pots, or sprigs of branches and cut flowers can be used.

Do not underestimate the energetic effects from the aroma of the food you produce. It is a wise piece of advice that, if selling your house, you should bake some bread, as this makes potential buyers subconsciously more inclined to purchase.

Another way you can control the aroma within a dwelling is with the use of fruit. Citrus fruits such as lemon and apples can provide a stimulating and fresh energetic atmosphere; peaches produce an aroma that promotes health. It is most important to use fresh and undamaged fruit if you wish to create aromas with specific energetic effects. If fruit is not eaten quickly it should be disposed of.

Scented candles, oils and incense are yet more tools for exercising control over the aroma environment within your dwelling.

Adjusting the circulation of chi
Smells of a yang nature will tend to promote circulation of energy, while yin-natured smells will tend to reduce it. This can be seen in the specific effect of aroma on people. Lavender has a yin effect, making you tend to slow down and relax; musk and cinnamon invigorate; smelling salts have long been used to shock people back into consciousness.

Adjusting the quality of chi
When an environment smells good to you this is generally indicative of good chi. Compare your response to the smell of food cooking to the smell of decaying food, or your reaction to the smell of burnt food. Fresh, pleasant smells are good; a foul, noxious aroma should be removed by elimination at its source.

Symbols
You might think it would be difficult to create symbols of aromas but, in fact, pictures or ornaments with which you associate a particular aroma can be quite powerful. Those depicting roses and other strong-smelling flowers can be used; in the kitchen, try pictures of fruit or freshly baked bread.

Care needs to be taken when using artificial plants and flowers, which may symbolise certain aromas but often have their own distinct chemical smell. This could result in the actual rather than symbolic smell being stronger, thus having a negative effect. This is usually the case when they are made of plastic and are either relatively new or become heated, as when they are left standing in the sun. It is suggested that leaving newly acquired plastic flowers outside in natural daylight for a few days may get rid of most of these chemical smells. Dried herbs could also be placed in a vase containing artificial flowers, which would create additional beneficial aromas, but do not use this technique to mask otherwise unpleasant artificial smells.

Table 32 — Eliminating excess chi, deficient chi and stagnant chi conditions associated with aroma

ENERGY PROBLEM	ENERGY SOLUTION (ENHANCEMENT)	COMMENTS
EXCESS CHI	• Eliminate the source of burnt, scorched, acrid or overpowering smells.	Make sure that ovens and grill trays are kept fresh and clean, as these can otherwise be a continuing source of these smells.
DEFICIENT CHI	• Introduce sources of pleasant, fresh-smelling aromas.	Flower smells are the most commonly used but the smell of fresh pine, lemons and peaches can be particularly beneficial.
STAGNANT CHI	• Introduce aromas such as lemon and citrus which will move and disperse stagnant chi.	This effect can also be achieved with ammonia and other chemicals, often found in bleaches and detergents. These should be used warily as they are strong enough to introduce an excess chi element.

Table 33 — Adjusting aroma energy in accordance with personal energy objectives

ENERGY OBJECTIVE	ENERGY ENHANCEMENT	COMMENTS
INCREASE YANG	Introduce sources of stimulating, invigorating aromas into the environment.	These include cinnamon, ginger and lemon.

ENERGY OBJECTIVE	ENERGY ENHANCEMENT	COMMENTS
DECREASE YANG	Reduce sources of stimulating or invigorating aroma in the environment.	As above.
INCREASE YIN	Introduce sources of calming, relaxing aromas into the environment.	These include lavender, peach and pine.
DECREASE YIN	Reduce sources of stimulating or invigorating aroma in the environment.	As above.

Understanding how to interpret and deal with the special influences associated with your environment

This section looks at particular energy enhancement opportunities that arise in respect to the various components of the Feng Shui environment (introduced in Chapter 3). The:

• local area;
• land;
• buildings;
• rooms; and
• furnishings and fittings.

Where this material identifies energetic enhancements appropriate for you, these can be added to Form 4 on page 177.

Local area

There are various 'factors' associated with your local area that will provide a better understanding of the condition of chi in that area. These include the local:

• climate;
• geographical features (landforms);
• soil types;
• vegetation;

- buildings (including transport facilities and power plants); and
- roads.

Local climate
Climate has the number one energetic impact of the environment and should be foremost in your mind when you are selecting a place to live.

Climate consists of:
- sunlight hours;
- temperature;
- moisture; and
- air movement.

Most of these have been dealt with in terms of the eight energy conditions; however, there are a few additional points that need to be made about sunlight and air movement.

Recent publicity has made us aware of the dangers of excessive exposure to sunlight but inadequate exposure is just as important. The SAD syndrome has recently been identified, where insufficient exposure to sunlight has been found to result in depression, and fatigue. Next time there are seven or eight cloudy days in a row, notice how difficult it is to maintain a feeling of wellbeing.

People who need to increase their yang energy balance and who either live in a temperate or polar zone, experience extended periods of cloud cover or mist or spend a lot of time indoors may be particularly affected and should try to increase their exposure to sunlight. (People living in subtropical or high-altitude zones, or anywhere where ultraviolet light is likely to be a problem should make sure they are properly protected and try to shift outdoor activities to the early morning or late afternoon.) They should try to:
- increase the time spent outdoors;
- ensure that internal lighting is of the full-spectrum variety;
- allow as much natural light as possible into the dwelling or premises; and
- carry out activities that take place in the house in as much natural light, that is, close to windows and skylights, as possible.

People who are trying to decrease the yang energy in their lives and who live in temperate and polar areas should not assume that reversing the above actions is appropriate. In such situations it is unlikely that sunlight is a significant contributor to excess energy if you are taking appropriate precautions against UV.

In terms of air movement, special hints for moving or renovating are as follows:

- If there are storms or excessive wind movements in the area, buildings should be on the lee side of hills and mountains and should not be placed at the summit. If stagnant air is the main problem, build higher up and on the windward side. Avoid building deep in valleys.
- If there are storms or excessive wind movements in the area, windbreaks (either of trees, walls or fences) can be interposed between the building and the direction from which the wind comes. It is important that these windbreaks are sufficiently strong or appropriately designed to survive the extremes of wind, otherwise they may constitute an active danger to the building. For instance, bamboo windbreaks will slow all but the strongest winds and rather than becoming airborne missiles when overwhelmed, are simply flattened against the ground.
- Buildings should be appropriately strengthened to survive the most severe conditions likely to be imposed.
- If there are storms or excessive wind movements in the area, it is better to have large windows and doorways on the lee side of the building. If stagnant air is the main problem, these should be on the windward side.

Local geographical features (landforms)

Most would regard landforms and the influence which they have on the energy of the environment as being one of the main facets of Feng Shui. It is true that landforms can play an important role in environmental energy but they are only one factor. On average, cities constructed in areas which have stunning scenery appear no more successful than those in relatively mundane surroundings. So if you do not have a mountain, lake or river adjoining your property, it does not mean that you can't have good Feng Shui.

The landforms we will look at are:

- the ideal local landform;
- mountains and hills;
- deserts and plains;
- oceans and lakes;
- rivers and streams;
- waterfalls, marshes and bogs; and
- symbolic landforms.

The ideal local landform

If we could design the perfect Feng Shui location we would start with a horseshoe-shaped valley. The mountain at the closed end of the horseshoe would be the highest, with the left side of the valley (looking towards the open end) lower and the right side lower again. The slope of the mountain at the back of the horseshoe would not fall directly to the valley floor but flatten out to a small plateau about one-third of the way up. It is here that we would place our dwelling.

THE 'IDEAL' BUILDING SITE

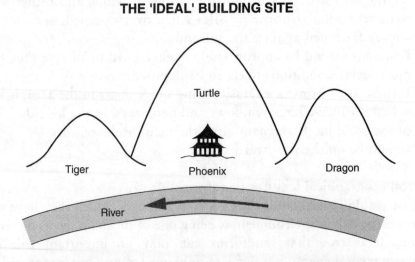

The house is on the plateau of a large mountain, which protects the rear of the house. A smaller mountain on the left (as you face forwards) protects the dragon side of the house and a smaller mountain again protects the tiger side. The front of the valley is open and contains a river bringing chi across the front of the house. In a hot climate the valley should face the closest of the poles; in a cold climate, the equator.

Down in front of the plateau a stream should cross from left to right. The open end of the horseshoe should face so that it allows both the morning sun to shine on the front of the house and entry into the valley of only the most favourable winds (moist, cooling breezes in a hot climate and warm, drying breezes in a cold climate). The mountain at the rear of the dwelling should shield it from unfavourable winds (strong, cold winds in a cold climate and strong, warm winds in a hot climate).

As you can imagine, there are few places on earth that meet these rigorous requirements. We can, however, draw from this description a set of preferred requirements.

1 The back of the property should be strong and stable, protecting the property from excess chi. This protection does not have to come from mountains, it can be from other buildings, trees, walls, etc.

2 The two sides of the property should also be protected, with the left (dragon) side predominating over the right (tiger) side (see the diagram opposite for explanations of dragon and tiger). Again, buildings, trees, walls or other structures may provide this protection.

3 The front of a building should face an open area of beneficial energy. Preferably, the building should face in the direction of the nearest water. If the back of your property rises steeply then it is obviously dangerous to have water at the back, as this would be likely to overflow towards your dwelling. If there is no such downward slope then water in the back garden is not such a problem.

4 The land on which the property is actually constructed should be flat and stable.

The more of these requirements the land around your property meets, the better Feng Shui it has.

If buying a property, you should look for the existence of as many of these as possible. If already the owner of a property, you should try to create such conditions around the dwelling by using walls, fences, trees, outbuildings, landscaping, etc. If you have a flat, or a property with a small garden, you should seek to satisfy as many of these requirements as possible by working directly on the energy structure of the dwelling itself.

Mountains and hills

From a Feng Shui perspective you can write books about mountains, their shapes and preferred formations — indeed, some people have. One piece of information you do need to know is that mountains are formed through either collision of crustal plates or volcanic upwelling. In this sense, their presence is indicative of yang energy. The higher the mountains and sharper the peaks, the more yang the environment will be. However, mountain building eventually ceases and the mountains then start to erode. This stage of a mountain's existence is much more yin. Mountain climates may also be very yin because of the cold and moisture involved, or yang because of the strong winds and harsh conditions.

We must also distinguish between the effects of living by mountains and living on mountains. Living by mountains may provide protection to valley dwellers from severe winds; mountains may also induce rainfall, and the deposition of materials eroded from their sides may make their lower slopes and adjoining regions rich and fertile. Living on mountains may expose you to those harsh conditions and strong winds.

Mountain shapes also represent the five elemental energies; therefore shape must be considered when evaluating the energetic impact of a mountain:

- Mountains that rise to a sharp point, or which are very craggy, represent the fire element. This would not be beneficial at the back of a property, as the fire and water elements would conflict. A view of such a mountain from the front window could be most beneficial — but not facing directly into the slope of the mountain.
- Mountains that are more columnar (with flattened top) represent wood energy.
- Gentle, curved, rolling hills represent metal energy.
- Squarish mountains represent earth energy.
- Irregular mountains of no obvious shape would represent water energy.

Deserts and plains

Deserts may be dry and hot, or cold and icy (as in the Tundra). The extreme nature of conditions tends to create excess chi of either a yin or yang nature. Plains have a similar distribution of extremes, plus the fact that they may be very fertile due to deposition of sediment after flooding (very significant in flood plains and deltas). This act of gathering is a particularly yin aspect.

Oceans and lakes

Oceans are generally dynamic, with surging currents and much active energy, while lakes are generally quiet and still. On a calm day, in protected areas, oceans may take on a lake-like nature. Likewise, large lakes can, on windy days, be surprisingly ocean-like. While permanent bodies of water are yin in respect to flowing water (as in rivers and streams), in this instance the ocean nature of water is yang, while the lake nature is yin. Look for the nature generally exhibited by the ocean or lake close to where you live to decide how the energy of the water will affect your energy.

Rivers and streams

Streams are generally active, alive with movement and the sound of splashing water. Rivers usually flow majestically, with only the movement of a leaf or twig showing their currents. Of course, in certain areas, streams widen out and become still and calm, while rivers can rage and roar over rapids and through canyons. Although moving bodies of water are yang in respect to permanent water (as in oceans and lakes), in this instance the stream nature of water is yang while the river nature is yin. Look for the nature generally exhibited by the stream or river close to where you live to decide how the energy of the water will affect your energy.

Be aware that large volumes of fast-moving water can be too much of a good thing, even if you wish to decrease yin or increase yang. Fast-flowing rivers near rapids and weirs create excess chi, as do large waterfalls. They can be invigorating to visit for a short time but can create problems if you live next to them. Consider large falls, such as the Niagara, Iguasu and Victoria falls. They are spectacular, but how often do you see large pictures of them on lounge-room walls? (However, pictures of lakes and mountain streams, or even mountain waterfalls, are quite common.) People instinctively recognise that these large waterfalls represent too much energy.

Waterfalls, marshes and bogs

Waterfalls generally represent almost a yang extreme of water, alive with movement and the sound of splashing water (but see above about excess chi associated with large waterfalls). Marshes and bogs, on the other hand, represent extreme yin, which can easily result in stagnant chi.

If you live close to a large waterfall and still feel that you need to increase yang energy, or live next to a bog or marsh and still want to increase yin energy, caution needs to be exercised. Rather than yin or yang being deficient, they might be, respectively, stagnant or exhausted. In such situations you would do better getting advice from a Feng Shui consultant, so no appropriate actions for these conditions are noted.

Symbolic landforms

Unfortunately, if you live in a city you often do not have any exposure to natural landforms. While other city buildings and roads may take the place of hills, mountains and streams, they do not fully replace them in the Feng Shui sense.

It can be beneficial to introduce these natural landforms, or symbols of them, into the property or dwelling. This can be done with pictures, including paintings and photographs, of natural landforms such as mountains, oceans, valleys, rivers, deserts and, perhaps, even caves.

Another interesting way of introducing natural landforms into the dwelling is by the use of a pot landscape — an arrangement of rocks, pebbles, gravels and sands (sometimes with water, mosses and small plants or bonsai) that evokes the imagery of various landscapes, such as mountain images, valleys and islands.

Local soil types

The more yin a soil, the more moist it will tend to be. In extreme yin conditions water will tend to lie on the surface and the ground itself will be sticky and clumpy. The more yang a soil, the drier it will be. In extreme yang conditions water will sink instantly into the ground, which will be sandy or dusty, tending to move with a light breeze.

Local vegetation

If you live in a town or city, the only vegetation that will concern you is the vegetation in your garden or house, unless you live next to a park or reserve. If living in the country, however, the type of vegetation in the general landscape can be a good indicator of the energy impact of the vegetation on you.

Yin vegetation tends to be soft with large, round leaves; yin trees are usually flexible, for example, willow and bamboo. Yang vegetation tends to be harder and drier, with smaller or spikier leaves; yang trees are inclined to be strong and wind-resistant, for example, pines and oaks. Gum trees are relatively yang.

Reading various texts to find out whether a plant is yin or yang can sometimes get a little confusing. You have to remember that no plant or anything else is yin or yang in itself, it is only yin or yang relative to other things. Thus, you can create a list of plants that are yin or yang, but you can divide that list into plants which are yin or yang in comparison to each another, and keep on doing this till you get down to two plants. This is why it is important to understand yin and yang properly, rather than relying on lists.

Local buildings

Buildings influence your energetic environment as much as any natural feature. We have already seen how nearby buildings can be used to simulate the protection of a dwelling that is created by hills and mountains. The key energetic aspects of buildings are related to their:

- shape;
- materials;
- function.

Shape

Buildings have a three-dimensional shape but the two most important factors are their vertical and horizontal elevations. The vertical elevation is what the building looks like face on, the horizontal elevation is how the building appears looking down from above.

It is important to realise that the shape in which you are interested in is the part of the building you own. If you live or have your business in a multi-storey building partly owned by others, the outside shape of the building is not as important as the shape of the part of the building that forms your dwelling or workplace.

- Wood buildings have a predominantly columnar shape. Many skyscrapers and high-rise buildings have this form.
- Fire buildings have a predominantly pyramid or cone shape. Few buildings that people live or work in are constructed in this way.
- Metal buildings have a predominantly hemispherical shape. Aircraft hangers are one example. These buildings are often used to store or manufacture physical items.
- Water buildings have no particular shape. Many modern shopping complexes are good examples of this type of building, as are some larger hospitals and schools.
- Earth buildings are predominantly cubical in shape. This describes many residential homes, which are much closer to the shape of a cube than they are to the shape of a column.

Fire buildings are more suitable for religious and spiritual practice; wood buildings support expansion and growth; metal buildings are good for businesses involving manufacture and distribution; water buildings are good for study and reflection; earth buildings have stability and security, and are extremely good as dwellings.

It is the basic shape of a building we are interested in. Adding a few gables and porches does not change the overall nature of the building. Most buildings will have different elements but the more pronounced one particular element is, the greater the energetic effects associated with that element will be.

Materials
The nature of materials used will also affect the energetic nature of the building. These effects can be classified in accordance with the five elements, as follows.

- Timber has (perhaps not surprisingly) a wood nature, as does paper (such as that used in Japanese buildings) and thatched and shingle roofs. Canvas and skins would also be regarded as wood.
- There are no fire construction materials, though, naturally, if

you use a red-coloured building material, you will be adding a fire element to the building. A fire element is also introduced into buildings with electrical wiring (when power is connected).
- Again, it is probably not surprising that steel, iron, aluminium, and so on, add a metal element to a building.
- Glass represents the water element.
- Earth elements are the main building materials, including, stone, brick, cement, tiles and ceramics.

Buildings will usually be a mix of materials with the predominant materials having the most energetic influence.

The more 'massive' the materials in relation to the size of the building — large stone blocks and columns, large timber beams — the more yin the building; the less massive the materials, the more yang.

Function

The function of a building will also affect its energetic impact. Basically, any building that has people going in and out of it is going to have a yang effect on the local environment. The busier these places are, and the more of them there are, the more yang the effect. Particularly, yang buildings are likely to be places of worship (but not places of religious retreat and contemplation), schools, retail centres, transport centres (such as railway stations, airports and ferry terminals), sporting complexes and entertainment venues.

There are buildings with functions which have a negative impact on the chi of the area, because they tend to result in stagnant or sha chi. These include garbage depots, incinerators, correctional institutions, medical facilities and hospitals, transport facilities, power stations and electrical installations, heavy manufacturing operations and abattoirs.

It is not practical to provide a list of solutions to all the energetic influences that variously shaped buildings with various functions might have on your environment. This would take a book in itself! The information provided above can, however, be useful to you, both as a way of assessing the likely energetic impact of a local building on a property you own, are contemplating living or working in, or are contemplating buying or renovating.

Local roads

Most buildings have a frontage to a road (unless they front on to water). The word 'road' must be understood in its original, rather than modern sense, that is, not just as an area given over to the transportation of motor vehicles but including any pathway or lane along which people or vehicles travel. Malls and arcades should therefore be considered as roads.

The chief considerations with roads are the volume of traffic (pedestrian and vehicular) and the speed at which that traffic is moving. This speed is relative. Pedestrian traffic speeding past at 6 km per hour is energetically faster than cars travelling at 50 km per hour. If you owned a shop in a mall you certainly would not want large volumes of people travelling quickly past your shop as this would make it difficult to attract them inside. Vehicular traffic going at 50 km per hour past a shop is no problem at all, although traffic travelling over 80 km per hour would be.

If you have read other Feng Shui books, you will be aware that facing a 'T' intersection or being on the outward side of a curve in the road are regarded as situations where excess chi may be generated. This is true on busy roads but may even be advantageous on quiet, suburban roads and lanes. This is because the chi in these areas may be a little too yin, and these positions may result in the chi becoming more yang without any risk of sha chi situations developing. What you have to look at is not the road configuration but the volume and direction of energy. The inside of a curve might be regarded as the best energetic condition, although I, for one, would not live in such a position if the road in question was a six-lane highway.

If you live on a road that does tend to result in excess chi, the best solution is to deflect this by building walls and/or vegetation screens. Be particularly aware of the need to curve paths and driveways so that they do not provide a free run for the excess chi direct from the road to your premises.

If a road slopes down towards your property this speeds up the flow of chi. Road configurations which require abrupt changes of speed, such as those adjacent to traffic lights, also result in excess chi.

Land

To assess the energetic impact of land which you own or are proposing to buy, you need to consider the following aspects of it:
- shape;
- slopes and changes in height; and
- the eight energy conditions.

Shape
The five elements apply to the shape of land.
- A square block represents earth nature energy and is considered most beneficial.
- A rectangular block represents the wood element. This is also a good shape, but it is preferable that the longest boundary be at the back of the property. A lot of suburban blocks are deeper rather than longer, but their basic shape is still wood. As a rough rule of thumb, a block takes on more of a wood nature when its longer sides are twice or more the length of its shorter sides.
- A triangular block represents fire. You would have to be careful with such a block, particularly if the apex of the triangle faced to the rear.
- A hemispherical block representing metal would be unusual, whether the curve was to the front or rear. It could be good for some businesses and workplaces.
- An irregularly shaped block would represent water. This would generally be good for such activities as farming and research. Again, it would be preferable if the larger side of the block were at the rear of the property.

The sides of a block of land can also be classified in accordance with the five elements. Classify the left and right sides of the property by standing with your back to the rear, looking towards the front. The five elements are each associated with a 'symbolic' animal, and when referring to directions in Feng Shui it is common to refer to the side of the property, building or room that we are talking about in terms of its symbolic animal (for example, the 'green dragon side'). Since each symbolic animal is representative of the five elements, you might wonder why we simply don't refer to the 'wood' side of a property. The reason is that there are many attributes which attach to the five elements, such as nature of smell and taste, that are irrelevant to the energy associated with each side of a property.

Using the names of the symbolic animals focuses us on the particular energetic attributes of the five elements that are relevant here when considering the 'sides' of property. Thus, the Green Dragon symbolises energy of change and growth. The Red Phoenix symbolises energy that renews and sustains us, and is associated with prosperity. The White Tiger symbolises assertive, or if it is too powerful, confrontational energy. The Black Turtles symbolises energy that protects us. The Yellow Snake indicates energy that grounds us and supports the other four energies.

- The front is the fire side and is symbolised by the Red Phoenix. This side is the energetic front of the property. The fire side should not dominate the rear (water) side; it should not be longer, higher or stronger. 'Stronger' and 'weaker' refer to the relative energetic strength of those areas of a property and, as such, cannot be defined. The type of things that would indicate them are a well-maintained front garden with bright reddish flowers (strong) and a neglected back garden (weak).
- The left side of a property is the wood side and is symbolised by the Green Dragon. This should not be dominated by the right (metal) side (it should not be shorter, lower or weaker).
- The right side of a property is the metal side and is symbolised by the White Tiger. As stated, this side should not dominate the left (wood) side.
- The rear side of a property is the water side and is symbolised by the Black Turtle. As stated, this should not be dominated by the front (fire).
- The centre of the property represents the earth element.

Slopes and changes in height

The lower side of land is yin in respect to the higher side. Preferably the rear and left sides of a property would not be lower than the front and right sides. If this is not the case and the difference in height is substantial, then the rear and left sides of the land will need to be strengthened energetically.

The eight energy conditions

When inspecting land or evaluating your own property do not forget to analyse the eight energy conditions, as described earlier.

Buildings

Rather than duplicate the information already detailed in 'Local buildings', this section will only deal with those additional aspects relevant to the building in which you live and/or work. For any aspects relating to the form or function of your building, please refer to the relevant sections.

The additional aspects dealt with here include:

* direction;
* state of repair; and
* energetic function.

Direction

A lot of Feng Shui books go into much detail about in which compass direction your house should face. We have already discussed in Chapter 1 why this is not particularly important. What is important is that the front of your house represents its 'face', and it is here that most energy should enter your dwelling.

If the front of your house has excess chi conditions, you will naturally seek to reduce or transform energy in this area; if it has deficient or stagnant chi conditions, you will be seeking to encourage the generation and movement of energy.

Split-level houses

There is nothing wrong with split-level houses in themselves; however, their design often results in a disturbed flow of chi. Making sure that chi circulates freely and evenly throughout such a property is important.

The state of repair of the building

Leaking gutters, peeling paint, frayed electrical wiring, etc., are all to be avoided, not only for their poor appearance and the dangers they represent but also because they are associated with stagnant chi.

The consistency of design of the building with basic energetic principles

The Chinese have always believed that the same principles operating in nature should be applied to building design. They therefore saw a dwelling as similar to a living organism and felt that the building should be designed to match the way in which an organism functioned.

The front of a building is its face. Just as living organisms have their mouths within their faces, so, too, the main door of a house or dwelling should be at the front of the building. Since the mouth is where a living organism takes in its food and air (we can ignore the nose for the moment), so, too, the front door has equal importance as the point of energy entry for a building.

The back of the building is like the back of an animal, a point that needs to be well defended to prevent surprise attack. Just as an animal when threatened will seek to protect its back while facing the threat, so, too, should a building face outwards to incoming energy, with the back protected.

We can draw other analogies between the systems of living organisms, such as circulatory, respiratory and neurological systems, and the features within a building. For example, an organism only continues to live if it can distribute the energy obtained from air and food to all the cells in the organism. In like manner, the energy taken in through the front door of a building needs to be distributed throughout that building. This is one of the reasons why the Chinese believed that having the front and back door of a building directly aligned is poor Feng Shui. In such a case, the energy that entered the building would proceed directly through it and out the back door, providing no 'energetic nutrition' to the building or its occupants.

The kitchen of a dwelling can be likened to the digestive system of an organism. Care must be taken that the digestion (cooking) can take place undisturbed. The digestion analogy also applies to the dining room and so, similarly, you must ensure that this area is relatively undisturbed. The bathroom and laundry can represent the eliminative organs of the building. Just as these organs are found at the rear of an organism, so, too, the bathroom and laundry should be placed close to the back of a building.

When an organism rests it is at its most vulnerable. For this reason, the sleeping quarters of a house or dwelling should also be placed to the rear of the building, be relatively well protected and out of any significant energy flows.

Rooms

To date we have looked at rooms simply as part of the structure of a house that allows you to finetune various Feng Shui enhancements that will move you closer to your personal energy objectives. This section identifies the energetic nature of the activities that take place in rooms and particular energetic aspects associated with these rooms. It is a little bit of a balancing act to have both the right chi energy in a room and pursue your personal energy objectives. The rooms we will look at are the:
- bedroom;
- kitchen;
- living room;
- laundry;
- dining room;
- bathroom and ensuite;
- study and home office;
- garage/home workshop/storeroom; and
- hall.

Bedrooms
Background
Bedrooms are one of the most important areas of the house. You may well spend more time in this part of the house than in any other, and the more time you spend in an area the more influence that area can have on you. Also, the bedroom is where you sleep, and proper sleep is vital to health. Finally, it is often a key area for relationships.

The energy requirements for sleep and relationships are quite different, so let's look at these separately.

Sleep
What you will be seeking to achieve in the bedroom is an energy environment that lets you fall asleep easily, sleep undisturbed, and

wake refreshed and invigorated. But let's remain grounded in reality. No one should expect to sleep perfectly each and every night, and wake up raring to take on the ascent of Mount Everest. What we are talking about are general sleep patterns. For instance:

- If you have difficulty going to sleep, toss and turn, and wake up at the slightest sound, this is a yang condition and you should try to reduce the energy level in your bedroom.
- If, on the other hand, you fall asleep right away, are difficult to wake, sleep long hours, and still wake up lethargic, this is a yin condition and you should look at increasing the energy level in your bedroom.

To make a yin or yang energy change in the bedroom, you can adjust any of the eight environmental energies as indicated in the tables contained in this chapter. In this case, replace your personal energy objective with your objective for the bedroom's energy, that is, to increase or decrease yin or yang.

There are a number of 'special' factors that are either unique to or particularly important in bedrooms in relation to sleeping. They include the following:

DISTURBED ENERGY INDICATORS	DISTURBED ENERGY SOLUTIONS
Mirrors in the bedroom — particularly where you can see yourself in the mirror from the bed. (Don't forget to look behind you.)	• Remove mirror entirely or cover it during sleep periods with screen or curtains. Note: Mirrored wardrobe doors can be a real energetic problem in bedrooms, especially for children. Consider reversing them, replacing one mirror door with a solid door and sliding the remaining mirror doors behind it at night, or slide them all up one end out of line of sight of the bed at night.

DISTURBED ENERGY INDICATORS	DISTURBED ENERGY SOLUTIONS
Your bed is directly aligned with a bedroom door or window, or both.	• Move the bed to a better alignment. • Place a screen or barrier between the bed and door or window. • Use heavy drapes or curtains that are closed over window at night. • Keep the offending door closed at night. Note: If you are going to move a bed, it is worthwhile looking at what is your most beneficial direction in which to lie. If you are already sleeping facing your most beneficial direction, look at using screens and barriers to solve problems rather than moving the bed.
Head of the bed is unsupported and/or immediately in front of window.	• Place head of bed against a solid wall. • Put solid bedhead or screen at head of bed. • If head of bed abuts window, have solid shutters on window that are closed during the night. Note: The lack of appropriate energy at the head of the bed has been included as disturbed energy because a simple movement of furniture can rectify the energy problem. Some of the other options do mention bringing extra items into the bedroom but this is not to change the level of energy in the bedroom as a whole.
Foot of bed faces door or window.	• Place a footboard at the foot of the bed, projecting above the level of the bed. • Place a solid object, such as a carved clothes box, at the foot of the bed. • Hang heavy drapes on the window and close them at night. • Use a screen at the end of the bed at night.

DISTURBED ENERGY INDICATORS	DISTURBED ENERGY SOLUTIONS
Excessive noise, light, temperature, moisture, moving energy or bio-energy conditions.	The solutions are the same as those detailed under the eight energy conditions but be particularly aware of the following: • Electrical equipment close to the bed should be reduced to a minimum. • High noise levels are a problem, especially if the noise is intermittent and unpredictable. • Avoid having anything hanging down over the bed, particularly heavy, sharp-edged ceiling beams. With the exception of moisture, most of these energies should be kept in a more yin condition than the rest of the dwelling.

Relationships

Relationship activity requires a much higher energy level than is appropriate for sleep. This means that you have to build a little controllability into your bedroom's energy environment that allows you to shift back and forth between appropriate energy levels.

- Lights will, of course, raise the energy level when turned on. If this light is of a pinkish colour it will support relationships; if you need to increase communication, think of introducing orange colours. Candles also have excellent effects.
- Music is an easy way of increasing energy levels in a controllable way, as are artificial fountains.
- You may need to pay attention to raising the temperature of the room as opposed to that of the bed, particularly in a cold climate. Artificial log fires powered by gas can introduce both light, heat and movement into a bedroom.

General observations

It is probably self-evident that the energy of a bedroom is more likely to be appropriate if it exists as a separate room. An important point to remember, however, is that the bedroom does not have to exist as a separate room all the time. For instance, traditional Japanese architecture often delineates an area of a building for living purposes during the day, transforming it into a sleeping room at night. The important thing is that, once the area is used for sleep, it conforms with the energy requirements for that activity.

Observant people will note that the Japanese futon not only has no energetic support at the back of the head but is also placed in the centre of the room (so the head cannot rest against a wall). This may have been that because of the flimsy nature of rice-paper partitions, security was actually enhanced by the bed being in the centre of the room. Note, also, that with a futon the head is not raised any substantial height above the floor. Thus, the sense of space behind the head is not particularly great.

A bedroom can be too big. Having acres of space around the bed creates as many problems as having the bedroom too small or enclosed, because it increases the yang nature of the room's energy, making it difficult to sleep. It is also best not to have items hanging over the head while you sleep.

Kitchens

The kitchen is where we prepare food and this makes it one of the most important rooms in the house. The energy in this part of the house will affect the food you eat. It is most important that the kitchen be free from stagnant chi. There should therefore be good ventilation and plenty of light.

Kitchens are sometimes seen as problems because they contain both 'Fire' and 'Water' elements and these elements are seen by some as being in opposition. (However, see 'Five Elemental Energy Phases' on page 86, where it is shown that you can just as well see the elements as controlling each other). The truth is that all environments will contain aspects of the five elements. Even our bodies manage to get along with the Kidney water element and Heart fire element.

The traditional Chinese kitchen did not of course contain fridges, electric cookers, dishwashers etc. What they did have were open-mouthed combustion fires and containers of water. Obviously no good was going to come of bringing these items together. In our modern kitchens the most probable threat is bringing electricity (a fire element) in contact with water.

This means that while we still need to be cautious about how we control the meeting of fire and water elements in the kitchen, we do not need to go overboard just because they are both present.

Hotplates, ovens, stoves and any heating devices represent the fire element. Fridges, sinks, dishwashers and freezers represent the water element. To minimise any potential conflict between fire and water elements do not place them directly opposite each other. If this cannot be avoided then ensure there is a wood element between them. This could be a table or wooden floor or even an indoor plant.

One point to remember in your Feng Shui reading is that when reference is made to the mouth of a stove having to be protected from water, the mouth is not where we put the food in but where we put the fuel in. In electric and gas stoves this as at the back of the stove so the 'mouth' is protected.

Another problem common to kitchens is the number of sharp-edged implements and knives that may be present in the room. It is better that these be put away in drawers or knife blocks, as they may otherwise cause excess chi.

Living rooms
Living rooms are places of activity and communication, and are therefore of a yang nature. Whatever your personal energy objectives might be, it is best from a family perspective to leave this room reasonably yang.

Dining rooms
At first glance it may seem that dining rooms should be yin areas to support digestion and this is basically true. However, dining rooms are also areas where families communicate and this is a yang activity. Therefore, while we should seek to avoid very yang environments we should not make the dining area too yin. Using a little orange in the dining room (perhaps using pictures, paint, tablecloths, curtains, rugs, carpets, table mats or table decoration) can help to stimulate conversation. In open-plan dining areas try to make sure that there are not energetic distractions such as TVs, computers, or loud and rhythmic music.

Bathrooms and ensuites
The nature of most bathrooms is yin, due to the water nature of the activities that take place therein. However, the bathroom does not

have to be yin and you can work on creating as much energy as you like in this area. You can, for instance, make sure that the area is bright, light, colourful and dry.

Ensuites can be a problem, with their close proximity to the bedroom. It is best that the door between the ensuite and the bedroom open inwards to the ensuite and be kept closed when not in use.

The study and home office

If the study is a place for gaining knowledge then its energetic condition should be yin. If the study is a place where business is carried out, or where decisions are taken and strategies planned, then the energetic background should be yang.

Where there are customers and clients visiting the home office, it should preferably have a separate entrance and be at the front of the house.

Garages/home workshops/storerooms

These are often places where things are stored. Even with home workshops, a lot of the time they are simply places to keep tools, repair materials and unfinished projects. As such, the places are yin in nature. The greatest danger, energetically, is that there will be stagnation of chi. It is best to make sure that these areas are kept tidy and clean, with periodic clean-outs of all those things no longer needed or used.

Furniture and fittings

We have already discussed most of the major appliances and furniture items, such as beds, wardrobes, fridges, airconditioners, fans, combustion heaters, sinks, dishwashers, televisions, computers, ovens and artificial lighting. However, the following are also worth discussing.

Clocks

It is not unusual to have clocks around the house that are either broken or do not keep good time. Like any other broken item they represent stagnant chi and should be repaired or thrown out. They can be more important than most broken items because we continually look at clocks to assess the time, whether they are broken or not. This increases their energetic impact and our feeling that things are not being well maintained.

Bonsai plants

Properly kept bonsai plants are regarded as having powerfully concentrated chi energy and will have a more energising effect than will normal plants. Some Feng Shui practitioners have reservations about bonsai because their natural growth is contained. To me if you follow this logic you should be equally concerned about mown lawns and any plant that is trimmed and pruned. Clearly the traditional Chinese had no problem with such activities — as evidenced by the large number of paintings of bonsai in place in various sage's gardens. One must also recognise that any aquarium contains 'bonsai fish' because their natural growth is constricted to a size appropriate to the amount of water available to them. In fact the same argument could indicate that we get rid of all pets because they certainly do not live 'natural' lives with us.

Of course 'natural' is all a matter of perspective. Many species have developed forms of dependence that are mutually beneficial but that modify the original 'natural' behaviour. Scientists call such mutually beneficial relationships 'symbiotic'. Who is to say that our keeping 'pets' is not a 'natural' symbiotic relationship? The same argument applies to maintaining a garden or keeping an aquarium.

My feeling is that well-developed bonsai represent the essence of larger trees in the same way that some rocks may call mountain ranges to mind. The care and love that is lavished on bonsai also creates beneficial energy.

Dried flower arrangements

You may also hear that dried flowers are not good Feng Shui because they are the dead remnants of living things. If we accepted this logic we would be reduced to environments made of minerals or artificially manufactured substances. Gone would be products made from timber, cane, ivory, paper, wool, cotton, chalk and all rocks composed of the remains of the bones and shells of living creatures. If we can sleep on a wooden bed between the dead remnants of plant material (sheets and blankets) in a wallpapered room (and I have never heard any Feng Shui expert advise to the contrary), I do not think you have too much to worry about with a few dried flowers. In fact, they are one way of introducing plant bio-energy symbols.

Stone columns
These can symbolise strength and support and are useful for building yin. (Some care should be taken in using broken columns reminiscent of ruined temple buildings as these can also indicate stagnant chi.)

Form 3 — Personal program for elimination of identified excess chi, deficient chi and stagnant chi conditions

ENVIRONMENT _____

DATE ANALYSED _____

ENERGY CONDITION IDENTIFIED	DESCRIPTION OF CONDITION	SOLUTION IMPLEMENTED
EXCESS CHI CONDITIONS		
DEFICIENT CHI CONDITIONS		
STAGNANT CHI CONDITIONS		

Form 4 — Personal Feng Shui program

DATE OF ANALYSIS _____

LIFE ENERGY	ENERGY OBJECTIVE	SOLUTION IMPLEMENTED	DATE
CAREER OR MISSION			
INNER KNOWLEDGE			
FAMILY/HEALTH			
WEALTH AND ABUNDANCE			
REPUTATION AND FAME			
RELATIONSHIPS			
CAREER/CHILDREN			
HELPFUL PEOPLE AND ENVIRONMENTS			

Chapter 5

Developing Your
Feng Shui Skills

Introduction

The deeper your knowledge and understanding of Feng Shui, the more effective your use of the positive Feng Shui program will be. As indicated in earlier chapters of this book, for ease of reference the information provided in this chapter is divided up into notes.

Note 1   The interrelationship of Feng Shui and other chi living skills
Note 2   Compass directions and accounting for hemispheres
Note 3   Harmonising the relationship of major life activities
Note 4   Dealing with conflicting Feng Shui requirements of family members and other occupants
Note 5   Determining the relative impact of Feng Shui enhancements
Note 6   Personal numbers, stars and elements
Note 7   *Ba gua* diagrams
Note 8   *Ba gua* and the eight major life energies
Note 9   Historical development of Feng Shui
Note 10   The internal chi environment
Note 11   Geopathic stress and earth rays
Note 12   Ghosts
Note 13   When to use a Feng Shui consultant
Note 14   Fortune tables
Note 15   Using crystals

Note 16 Symbolic meanings of plants
Note 17 Designing 'colour schemes'
Note 18 Using mirrors
Note 19 Managing mobile phones, waterbeds and electric blankets

Note 1 — The interrelationship of Feng Shui and other chi living skills

Many readers will have come across the term 'chi kung' (*qigong*). In Chinese, 'chi' is 'energy' (see Note 3) and 'kung' means 'work' or 'skill'. Chi kung therefore translates as 'skill with' or 'working with' chi. (This term is usually used in a more limited sense, for example, as a synonym for either chi breathing, chi exercise or chi performance tricks — driving nails into wood with bare hands, rolling around on nails and glass, etc.) To the Chinese, any activity should be done with chi in mind, so, in this sense, whether cooking, exercising, writing, massaging, practising Feng Shui or whatever, we are working with chi. When using chi, we should use the same principles, practices and philosophies in whatever we do. In this sense, a common thread relates all activities.

There is a special group of activities which, when done as a chi kung, confer great benefit on the practitioner, either as a direct consequence of the generation and refinement of chi or because of the insights and chi skills generated within. These are referred to as the 'chi living skills'.

Along with Feng Shui they include:
• chi breathing;
• chi nutrition/diet;
• chi acupressure/massage;
• chi meditation;
• chi exercise; and
• Tai Chi.

Chi breathing
When we breathe in air we are taking part of the environment within ourselves. Naturally, we also take along the chi associated with that part of the environment. Chi breathing deals with the techniques for ensuring we obtain maximum benefits from this chi. Also included

are breathing techniques that, through chi circulation, enhance the state of health and relaxation of the body.

Chi nutrition/diet

When we ingest food we again take in chi. Chi nutrition includes not only techniques for extracting the most chi from the food but also techniques for selecting food with high quantities and qualities of chi, along with storing, preparing and cooking the food in ways that enhance the chi content — ensuring you get the right type of chi. This involves analysing your chi requirements, whether your diet needs to be predominantly of a yin or yang nature and how to balance the five elemental energy natures of foods, as well as the influence of herbs and spices on chi and how to use these therapeutically.

Chi acupressure/massage

Chi flows throughout the body via a network of channels and meridians known as the *ching lo* or *jing luo*. Pressure and massage techniques can either sedate or stimulate the flow of chi, as well as remove blockages. There are techniques both to use on yourself and on family and friends. These focus on health maintenance and are pleasant to experience and easy to learn.

Chi meditation

These are techniques for encouraging the flow of chi throughout the body. They involve positive visualisation combined with ancient Taoist techniques for mentally leading the flow of chi.

Chi exercise

Chi exercises are designed to encourage the flow of chi throughout the body, and, because of this, are also very good at relieving stress and tension. There are exercise systems such as Lotus Qigong (a body toning and relaxation system), Eight Golden Treasures and Tao Yin, amongst others.

Tai Chi

Tai Chi combines techniques from chi breathing, chi exercise and chi meditation with chi internal massage techniques to produce a sophisticated health management system that is a delight to perform.

Note 2 — Compass directions and accounting for hemispheres

The problem

Many Feng Shui practitioners (particularly in the Northern Hemisphere) place a great deal of stress on the importance of compass directions and the association of these directions with various energetic effects, such as cold and yin energy being associated with north, heat and yang energy with south. Obviously, these energetic associations are inverted in the Southern Hemisphere, and Feng Shui practitioners here have suggested that the associations with compass directions should also be inverted when applied in the Southern Hemisphere.

Practitioners in the Northern Hemisphere have ridiculed this argument, pointing out that if a house were situated on the equator then the energy associations would reverse halfway through the house. However, this simultaneously destroys the Northern Hemispherists argument. After all, if a house were built directly over the North Pole then all walls of the house would face south; if at the South Pole, all walls would face north.

Some Feng Shui practitioners go one better and believe that the compass directions have some real direction in space. They forget that, since the earth revolves, the east and west sides of the house face in opposite directions in space every 12 hours.

Because of these disputes, two major schools of thinking have formed. What we might call the 'directions' school, based primarily in China and other parts of Asia, places great stress on the importance of directions and their universality of meaning. The compass direction in which a house faces is important in itself, as well as the alignment of the eight major life energy centres being direction based. What we might call the 'chi' school believes it is the nature of energy received from a particular direction that is important. The eight major life energy centres are aligned to the energetic mouth of the house.

Anyone new to Feng Shui might suppose there is only one right answer — either one or both schools of thought are wrong but only one school can be right! How, then, can both schools point to success with their methods? I suspect the answer lies largely in the fact that energy of direction is only one aspect of Feng Shui. We have already pointed out that the energy of the environment is influenced by many factors and that in Feng Shui what we do is literally push the balance of these factors in a positive direction. It may turn out that, in the grand scheme of things, direction is really not of great importance.

Some people, however, may be interested in following the arguments involved. For this reason I have gone to some length to indicate why the Feng Shui Academy of China takes the approach it does.

The 'traditional' argument

The 'directions' school makes much of the fact it is practising 'traditional' Feng Shui and that any departure from the wisdom of the ancients is bound to be flawed. I dislike such arguments because they involve dogma rather than logic and reason. (Western medicine stalled for 500 years because no one was allowed to challenge the errors made by Galen, a Greek physician, 130–200 AD, who was the first to study physiology and anatomy based on observation rather than supposition. A founder of modern medicine, his reputation was such that he became the indisputable authority for centuries after his death. Unfortunately this also perpetuated a number of errors and misconceptions.) There is also some argument over whether directions were all that important in the 'traditional' approach. Let's look at some of the history of Feng Shui.

Feng Shui began with what is known as the 'landform' school. Basically, the features of the land were seen as representing the underlying chi. Feng Shui was carried out in a somewhat poetic manner, with those practising it seeking to locate dragons, dragon veins and various parts of the dragon's anatomy as represented by landforms. This school also tended to view an actual house as a living organism, with mouth (front door), digestive organs (kitchen) and eliminative organs (bathing and toilet areas).

As Feng Shui became more popular and moved down from the mountains into the plains, the absence of clear geographical features made Feng Shui much more difficult. Over time, a tool known as the *lo pan* was evolved. This is often described as a compass but locates much more than the magnetic compass direction. There are often up to twenty-four scales on this compass, with all scales directed at determining various chi influences. The magnetic directions are probably the easiest to understand and have become associated with the 'compass' school. In fact, the compass school works out very complex interactions between all the various scales.

The use of the eight major life energy areas of the *ba gua* is a modern technique, therefore it cannot play a role in the traditional argument. You can see from the above that either school could make a good claim to being the traditional school, so we'll leave arguments of precedence behind and start applying a little logic and reason.

What are compass directions?
We all know that compass needles point north, right? Wrong. Compass needles align themselves with the nearest geomagnetic line of force, which, although flowing in a generally northerly direction, are not straight lines, being distorted by natural factors such as the ore bodies within the earth and artificial magnetic fields (such as are created around electrical installations and transmission lines). The earth's magnetic lines of force are also dependent on the structure of the earth's magnetic field, which is always changing and may vary significantly during solar storms.

If you wander along with a compass in your hand, following the needle, you will eventually end up around the north polar area. (As you get to the polar area, the needle will swing around wildly and cease to be of much use!) However, your route to this area will be far from a straight line. At any particular point on your journey the compass needle may point slightly north-east or north-west. A compass, then, is fine for determining the *overall* direction in which you are travelling but is not a very accurate way of determining, at any one place, which direction is north. Concluding which way a building is aligned by taking a compass reading is fraught with inaccuracy.

How accurate is a compass in your local area?
To determine this you may like to perform the following experiment. From the building you live in, look out of a window with a northerly aspect and note the point on the horizon to which the compass needle points. Now, still viewing from the same window, select a place just outside your building which is on a straight line between where you are standing and the point you have just noted. Go outside to the

place selected and take a second compass reading. You may now find that the compass is pointing to a different spot on the horizon. If both spots are the same, then compass directions are probably pretty accurate and you can rule out localised disturbances in the direction in which the compass is pointing. To be sure, you should take a third reading about a kilometre further along that line to the horizon. If the spot on the horizon changes then you know there are local disturbances. Bear in mind that, in this case, neither of the two spots pointed to are necessarily due north.

Two-dimensional thinking

More confusion sets in because we get in the habit of thinking that our two-dimensional diagrams of compass directions are a real representation of what happens in three-dimensional space. For convenience, we all represent the four directions as straight lines 90° apart. However, the surface of the earth is curved, and so our diagram should use curved lines. If we now extend the lines far enough, north meets south and east meets west, just as it does in the real world. What a different picture we now have of the cardinal directions!

Understanding why energy should be different in different directions

If, from the time you were born, you were told that the colour others think of as green was called red and the colour red was called green, then you could argue forever that grass was red, without being persuaded. The argument would centre on the label given to a particular colour and would have nothing to do with the colour itself. If, however, it was understood that colours were different frequencies of light, agreement could soon be reached that both parties were talking about grass having the same frequency of light but that each one was giving this a different label.

I suspect that much of the argument over direction boils down to the same thing — arguing not about the underlying facts but over the labels given. These labels, north, south, east and west, convey no real information about underlying energy. Let's see if we can use different labels for directions, that convey more meaningful information.

We will start by replacing the term 'east' with 'spinward' and the term 'west' with 'anti-spinward'. Spinward is the direction in which the planet is turning and thus the direction from which the sun rises. Anti-spinward is the opposite direction to which the world turns, the direction in which the sun sets. Now we can ask ourselves: 'What is different about these two directions that could have some energetic impact?'

In the case of earth (and of most planets), spinward means that in the morning the 'east' side of a house will be turning into the direction from which the light and the solar wind are coming — the sun. In the afternoon, the 'west' side of the house is getting the light and solar wind as it is moving away from the sun. Due to the speed of the earth's revolution, at the equator the light hitting the 'east' side should be some 42,000 km per hour faster than that hitting the 'west' side! But wait, the speed of light in the universe is constant for any observer, no matter what speed the observer is travelling at in respect of the light source. To put it simply, nature gets around this problem by keeping the speed of light constant but changing the perceived wavelength.

Thus, by moving away from the labels 'east' and 'west', we can get deeper understanding of energetic differences that are not obvious in compass terminology. Can the same be said for the 'north' and 'south' compass directions? Here we can identify two potential effects.

First we have a magnetic North Pole and a magnetic South Pole. Geomagnetic energy certainly has direction. Energy flows upwards from the positive magnetic pole in the south, to the negative magnetic pole in the North Pole. Equating north/south with magnetic directions would definitely indicate that this energy is consistent in direction across the globe (given the local variations in direction of geomagnetic lines of force previously discussed). At the poles, the geomagnetic lines of force do not disappear but go downwards, through the centre of the planet, which is why compasses will not work in the polar areas. (The compass does, of course, work but it has to be turned on its side — not much use when trying to find out where you are going!) In theory, the energy effects that would have related to the north and south directions in a house at the equator are now found in the floor and ceiling respectively of a dwelling. This is an interesting Feng Shui problem if we are saying that magnetic lines of force have a major impact on an individual's Feng Shui.

Also consider polar and equatorial directions. The poles are cooler, with influences from this direction tending to be yin; the equator is hottest, with influences tending to be yang. The 'equator' side of a house therefore receives different energy to the 'polar' side of a house. We will call these the 'thermal' directions. (We must also recognise that the direction of prevailing winds, and the presence of large bodies of water and geographical features such as mountains and deserts, could significantly vary the thermal patterns.)

Where you are deficient in yang or have excess yin, it would always make sense to face in the equatorial direction to compensate for this energy condition. At the poles, hotter is downwards towards the centre of the earth and colder is upwards in the direction of space, so for 'thermal' direction we have a similar situation to geomagnetism, where the energetic effects of the north and south sides of a building are replaced by the floor and ceiling!

Perhaps, then, both schools of Feng Shui are each partly right and partly wrong. Geomagnetic energy effects don't reverse as the equator is crossed but thermal effects tend to do so (although this is not an abrupt reversal but a gradual one, as a person moves towards the equator).

If this is correct, then testing the various 'success rates' of the 'directions' school and the 'chi' school should show that if the former is used in the Southern Hemisphere, the success rate should be somewhat less than the success rates for the same techniques used in the Northern Hemisphere, and that this variation discrepancy should grow as you move southwards. The only problem with this type of test is, how could variations in the success rates due to the different techniques be isolated from those due to, for example, the competence of the practitioner? I suspect it would be difficult to produce a statistically conclusive test.

Once we get away from compass directions to directions in general, we can see there are a number of other directions that could have important energy implications, that is, upwards and downwards, or towards and away from the gravitational centre of the planet. From the point of view of dwellings this can generally be ignored — the floor is the floor and the ceiling is the ceiling! (There may well, however, be implications for space-based structures.)

Also, in terms of yin/yang, the altitude at which you live will have significance. A unit on the first floor of a forty-storey building may be identical in structure and direction to one on the thirty-ninth floor, but I would argue that their Feng Shui would be very different. Similarly, the Feng Shui of a shop three floors underground would be different from one in the same building three storeys above ground, even if they were structurally identical. Maybe, therefore, we should start talking about altitude above core level rather than sea level. Gravity and pressure increase towards the gravitational centre and decrease as we move away. (The Chinese were particularly concerned about *tien* chi, that flowing from heaven or above, and earth chi, that flowing from below, but in most modern Feng Shui this only seems to come out in astrological terms.)

Revolution direction of the earth around the sun, and the sun around the galactic centre may have an energy effect but this can probably be ignored for all practical purposes.

The Feng Shui Academy of China accounts for energy impacts of the following 'directions':

• spinward (old east);
• anti-spinward (old west);
• magnetic north;
• magnetic south;
• polar (direction of nearest pole);
• equatorial (direction of equator);
• upwards (direction outwards from the earth's centre — altitude); and
• downwards (direction inwards to the earth — altitude).

This set of directions can be applied to establish directional Feng Shui energy influences on any building or structure, including mines and underground dwellings, whether located on earth, another planet or in space itself.

For those who want to know if Feng Shui requires a geomagnetic field, the answer is, no, it's only one element to consider. Earth's own geomagnetic field drops to zero periodically, just before a reversal of the magnetic poles. Mind you, we could expect this to be associated with some very dramatic events.

Summation

All of this is not something about which the average person need be greatly concerned. Chinese doctors and Western doctors both have the ability to cure people, even though the underlying theory of what they do is different. The same is true of Feng Shui. The above will become important when we start building habitats on other planets. Feng Shui practitioners, however, should develop a theoretical understanding of how Feng Shui works if they are to progress in the art.

Note 3 — Harmonising the relationship of major life activities

You might be wealthy and successful but with few, or poor, relationships. On the other hand, your life may be full of rich relationships but your efforts within the family, the community, or at work go unrecognised. These are all indications that the energies of your major life activities are out of balance. What you have to evaluate here is whether you simply need to build energy in certain life areas or whether energy overly concentrated in one area needs to be redirected. If you are working eighty hours a week, no amount of extra energy in the relationship area is likely to fix the problem.

The beauty of the positive Feng Shui program is that it continually refocuses you on the eight major life energies. In that sense, by simply following the program, you will tend to do the things that will help rebalance these.

Note 4 — Dealing with conflicting Feng Shui requirements of family members and other occupants

If some people living in a building need to increase yang or yin and others need to decrease yang or yin, what do you do? People tend to get very concerned about this, worried that somebody's interests have to be sacrificed. This is not the case. The fact is that people have different requirements in many areas, including the food they need, how much sleep they must get and the amount of attention they require. We usually find no difficulty in accommodating such varying needs, as long as we are aware of them.

Regard your dwelling as you would a larder or fridge, but as full of different energies rather than different foods. With food there will be many common requirements but some individuals will eat more or less of one thing; others will supplement their diet with vitamins; some will drink fruit juice, others water, tea or milk.

Likewise, it is necessary to make sure your dwelling has a basically healthy energy diet available to all, with some energy supplements that occupants can take to meet their own individual requirements. This is not as difficult as it sounds. If different parts of your dwelling provide different types of energy, then, just as the occupants have their special foods, they will have special places in the dwelling where they feel comfortable. If individuals have their own rooms then these rooms should reflect their owner's special energy needs. Even when people share rooms they have their own bed, or their own side of the bed! With a little thought it is usually not difficult to locate areas in a dwelling favoured by a particular person and make this area support their special energetic needs.

One area of particular importance is the kitchen environment. Where family members have varying energy needs, this area should be set up to suit the 'chief' cook. The whole family will benefit when the cook is performing at an optimum level and enjoys being in the kitchen, rather than being grumpy, short-tempered and not being able to wait to get out. Studies, craft rooms, a person's favourite corner or chair — all offer possibilities for those who need special Feng Shui energy supplements.

Note 5 — Determining the relative impact of Feng Shui enhancements

Why should small, but nearby, changes in your environment have more effect than larger, more distant changes? This is a critical concept in Feng Shui and it has a scientific and logical basis. Let's consider that each of us is affected by the gravitational pull of Mars and the rest of the planets but, all in all, the effects of these gravitational fields do not influence our lives too much. The gravitational fields that do have a strong influence on us are those of the earth, the moon and the sun. From this we can deduce that there are two factors to consider when determining how environmental energy affects us. These are the power of the energy field and its distance from us.

All the energies that we know of (that operate at the macrocosmic rather than subatomic level) obey what is known as the 'inverse square' law. Set off a firecracker in your hand and you will suffer serious injury; set one off a few metres away and it will simply make a loud noise; at a couple of hundred metres distant you would probably not even notice it. For everyday purposes this can be understood as saying that the effects of energy decrease much more rapidly than the distance between the energy source and the object it is acting on increases. Conversely, the effect of the energy increases much more rapidly than the distance between the energy source and the object it is acting on decreases. A simple consequence of this law is that the electric field of the light bulb over your head will influence you a lot more than the electric field of a power station a kilometre away. This is so, even though the power station generates enough power to light tens of millions of light bulbs.

Note 6 — Personal numbers, stars and elements

Personal numbers, stars and elements are a Chinese shorthand way of deciding what your energy needs are likely to be. This is often practised in a way similar to the magazine approach to Western astrology — if you know which year and month you were born, then you know you're going to make a great lawyer and marry a Pisces! It seems to work for some people but it is not part of the positive Feng Shui approach.

The underlying theory behind these systems is actually quite logical and sophisticated. We have already discussed the fact that chi goes through various cycles (or seasons). This is as true on a cosmic scale as it is on lower-level scales, and people born at one point in that cycle will tend to reflect aspects of the chi energy existing at that time. What these systems provide us with is more information that may be useful in moving us towards being able to balance our energy correctly, but it is only one of many factors. As in Western astrology, proper calculations are quite complex and best performed by somebody who has been correctly trained. It is not simply a matter of reading your year of birth off a table!

Note 7 — *Ba gua* diagrams

The literal translation of *ba gua* (*pa kua*) is the 'eight diagrams', reputedly developed by the Emperor Fu Hsi (2852 BC) from the markings on a tortoise shell. The *ba gua* diagram consists of sets of three lines known as trigrams. Broken lines represent yin and unbroken lines represent yang, as shown in the diagram.

There are eight possible arrangements of yin (broken lines) and yang (unbroken lines). These arrangements describe the major combinations of yin and yang energy encountered in nature. They are arranged into a *ba gua* diagram, as shown below.

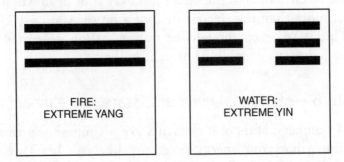

(These eight trigrams were later doubled to six-line constructions known as hexagrams, of which there are sixty-four possible arrangements. These hexagrams became the basis of the *I Ching* (The Book of Changes), one of the most famous Chinese books. Since the pattern of the hexagrams represents the natural energy cycle of chi, you can use the *I Ching* both to identify the current energy state and to predict the next stage of energy evolution in any particular situation. As such, the *I Ching* is used as a book of divination — one that predicts the likely future course of events and the consequences of actions.)

Readers may have seen two 'arrangements' of the *ba gua* diagram. These arrangements use the same trigrams but place them in a different order against different directions. The 'traditional' arrangement, as created by the legendary emperor Fu Hsi, shows the energy arrangement in perfect balance and harmony. The 'modern' or later version (which dates back over 3000 years) shows the trigrams in their dynamic arrangement. Both arrangements are used in Feng Shui, but for different purposes.

THE EIGHT TRIGRAMS (traditional version)

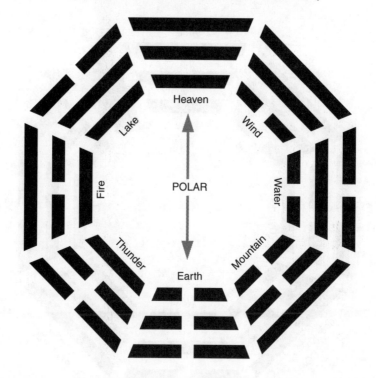

Use of the traditional *ba gua* on mirrors and with Tai Chi symbols
The most commonly seen use of the 'traditional' arrangement of the
trigrams is when they surround a mirror (the *ba gua* mirror), or as a
Tai Chi symbol. The perfectly balanced arrangement of trigrams
symbolises harmonious chi. With a *ba gua* mirror, you can deflect or
ward off negative chi; with the Tai Chi symbol, the focus is on
transforming the negative energy so it becomes more positive.

**Use of the traditional *ba gua* with the five elements and eight
major life energies**
The traditional arrangement is also used in Feng Shui to relate the
five elements and the eight major life energies to the direction in
which a building or dwelling faces. (This is more fully dealt with in
Note 8.)

The relationship of the five elements to the eight directions is
shown below.

BA GUA AND THE EIGHT MAJOR LIFE ENERGIES

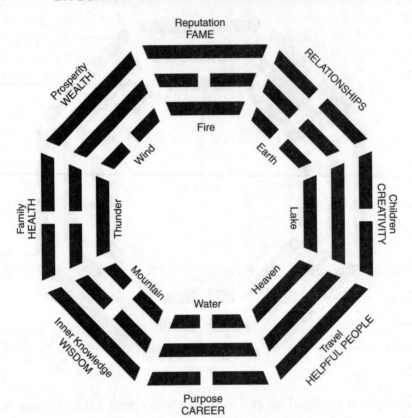

Use of the 'modern' (or later) *ba gua* trigram arrangement

This first version of the *ba gua*, referred to as the traditional *ba gua*, was later amended by King Wen of the Chou dynasty (circa 1200 BC). The purpose of this amendment was to reflect the cycles of chi as predicted within the *I Ching*. The modern arrangement of the *ba gua* is thus mainly used either to interpret future changes that may occur or to understand the reasons behind the existence of current situations.

Why is the top of the *ba gua* diagram shown as south and the bottom as north?

It is simply Chinese convention that south appears at the top and north at the bottom. One could speculate that since the *ba gua* diagram is fixed vertically on walls and gateposts (meaning that the trigrams are no longer aligned with compass directions), the use of the traditional arrangement becomes more appropriate, since the most yang trigram is at the top and the most yin trigram at the bottom. This reflects the yin/yang energies as they circulate between the earth (yin) and the remainder of the universe (yang).

Note 8 — *Ba gua* and the eight major life energies

The eight major life energies can all be related to different areas of a dwelling, room, business premises, office, desk or, indeed, any physical structure, as shown in the *ba gua* map below.

Ba gua relationships areas

WEALTH/PROSPERITY	FAME/REPUTATION	RELATIONSHIPS
Wood	Fire	Earth
Left rear	Middle rear	Right rear
FAMILY/HEALTH	TAI CHI	CHILDREN/CREATIVITY
Wood	Earth	Metal
Middle left	Centre	Mliddle right
WISDOM/ INNER KNOWLEDGE	CAREER/PURPOSE	HELPFUL PEOPLE
Earth	Water	Metal
Left front	Middle front	Right front

There are a number of things you need to know to be able to use this chart successfully:

- First, you must be able to align the chart with the 'direction' of your dwelling, room or other structure.
- Second, you must be able to 'fit' the chart to the land, building, room, or other area that has *ba gua* relationships you are trying to determine.

It is important to understand that the above chart does not anticipate a square dwelling composed of nine square rooms. It is intended to be a 'map' that you can place over a drawing of your building (or other area) to identify the places that most powerfully influence the eight major life areas. We are thus going to look at how to fit this map with your dwelling and at how to interpret the effect of areas of your dwelling which are either missing or extend beyond the map.

You can get very technical about 'fitting' the chart but you should remember that the only purpose of doing this is to identify the location of the life energy areas. A quite adequate identification of these can often be made from some very simple fitting techniques. Both simple and complex techniques are explained here, to accommodate those who feel better with '100 per cent' accuracy, but such increased accuracy will not make much difference to your Feng Shui.

Aligning the direction of a dwelling, room or other structure with the *ba gua* map

We talk about certain areas of a dwelling relating to wealth, relationships or any of the eight key areas of life energy. These associations are not arbitrary; they are based on the *ba gua*. However, note that one can use these eight associations without understanding the *ba gua* itself.

The eight major life energies can be aligned either to compass directions or with the major point at which chi energy enters the building or room. (The reasons for this are fully discussed in Note 2.) According to the Feng Shui Academy of China, they align with the energetic mouth of the building. According to this practice, the 'energetic front' of a house, room or desk is always the inner knowledge, career/purpose and helpful people areas, whereas the compass viewpoint is that these three aspects would always be on the north side of the house.

In line with the arguments presented in Note 2, where there is a clear energetic entrance to the building, I would say *ba gua* is aligned to this point; where there is no clear energetic entrance (as might occur in a modern shopping complex or other commercial development), traditional alignment with compass directions may be the only alternative.

The logic behind this interpretation of *ba gua* alignment is that the energy of compass direction is only one energy that influences the structure of the *ba gua* energy field, and that this may be overridden by strong chi flows from other sources, such as might be experienced through the energetic entrance to a building.

One other argument persuasive in discounting the importance of compass directions to *ba gua* is the situation in respect of waterborne dwellings. Many people spend virtually their entire lives on ships, houseboats, sampans, etc. It seems unreasonable that the *ba gua* of these dwellings changes every time their bows point in different directions.

Finding the energetic front of a dwelling

Once you understand the technique of aligning the eight major life energies with the energetic front of a dwelling, the next question that must be answered is 'Where is the energetic entrance to the building?' The best technique I have come across for locating such energetic entrances is to work out where a first-time visitor to a house would naturally go. People tune in on energy flows and where they go is the best guide.

It is the direction in which the energetic entrance faces that determines the front of your house. This is best explained diagrammatically.

If the door to the dwelling itself is not the external door, it is an internal door by which we enter the dwelling which determines the alignment of the *ba gua*, not the external door by which the *building* is entered. This would be the case for most flats.

Each level or storey of a building has its own *ba gua* map based on the direction of the energetic entrance to that level or storey. Thus, the *ba gua* alignment must be performed separately for each.

A house may be made up of separate dwellings, that is, a separate garage or self-contained flat, perhaps a separate workshop, studio or laundry. If the area has a roof separate from the main building, then the area should be regarded as a separate building and it will have its own alignment based on its own energetic entrance.

Fitting the *ba gua* map to a dwelling, room or structure

If you live in only part of a building, such as in a flat, the *ba gua* map is placed only over the areas you actually occupy, with one exception. You may have a room or area of a building that you have closed off or do not enter frequently, such as a guest bedroom, attic or storeroom. If you regard this area as yours then it should be

FRONT OF HOUSE FOR *BA GUA* PURPOSES

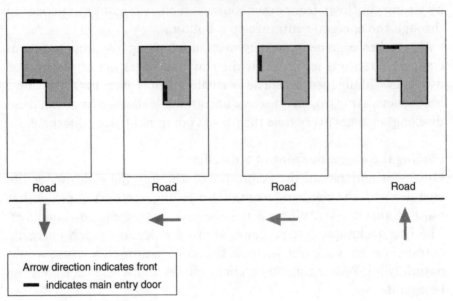

Arrow direction indicates front
— indicates main entry door

included. Communal areas should be ignored.

The first step is to draw up a *ba gua* map with the sides the same size (reduced to scale) as the floor plans of your house. Remember that you will need to draw up a *ba gua* map for each level or storey of your dwelling. If you have a split-level dwelling, where rooms are on different levels but no room is over the top of another, then treat the whole dwelling as being on one level.

If your dwelling/room is not square (very few are), you will need to work out the size of the area involved. If this is not included on any architectural plans, then usually the easiest way is to perform the following steps:

1 Measure the length and depth of the dwelling/area and multiply these figures to get the area in square metres.

Where you have an irregular shape, measure the length and depth of each 'missing' area, calculate the missing areas in square metres and deduct these from the total obtained above.

When you calculate the area, ignore separate buildings but include everything under your main roof, as long as it is 'enclosed' by walls.

2 When you have calculated the number of square metres for each level of your dwelling, take the square root of this figure (you will need a calculator). This square root figure will become the size of the sides of your *ba gua* map.

Naturally, you don't want actually to draw up a map the size of your house, so you will need to pick a scale. If you have architectural plans or have already drawn up a scale floor plan, then use the scale thereon. If not, choose a convenient scale such as 1:50 (where each metre of actual measurement is represented by 2 centimetres).

For example, if the area of your dwelling is 100 square metres, the length of your *ba gua* map would be 10 metres, which, on a 1:50 scale, would result in the sides of the map being 20 centimetres long. It is best if your *ba gua* map is on clear plastic, as you can then see exactly what is underneath each area when you overlay the map over the plan or diagram of your dwelling.

3 Place the *ba gua* map over the floor plans of your dwelling, trying to cover as much of your dwelling as possible. Some bits of your floor plan may stick out from under the map, while some parts of the map may cover space. This is not a problem, but has certain implications discussed later on.

If you have a particularly oddly shaped house (see diagram below) and feel that you cannot rely on your own judgment of which positioning of the *ba gua* map covers the greatest area of the house, then perform these additional steps:

1 Prepare another clear plastic sheet the same size as your *ba gua* map and rule off 1-centimetre scales.
2 Take a copy of your plans or diagram and shade all enclosed areas in a dark colour.
3 Place the plastic grid over the shaded plans and keep moving the plastic around until you can't reduce the number of clear squares any more.
4 Trace around the outside of the grid and then replace the grid with the *ba gua* map.

Some Feng Shui consultants advise that all of a building must be included in the grid. This is certainly a simpler technique but seems

DIFFICULT HOUSE SHAPES (FLOOR PLANS) TO FIT *BA GUA* MAPS

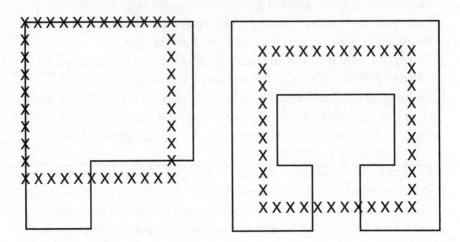

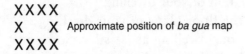

Approximate position of *ba gua* map

to presume that the shapes of dwellings can only create deficient areas — areas that will have a yin impact on a life energy area (a presumption that has no logical foundation that I can determine).

Reiteration of important points about the *ba gua* and eight areas of life energy

- The *ba gua* map does not assume your house is made up of nine square rooms. It is a grid reference to be placed over your house plan to show the major areas of influence. Each of the nine squares may contain various parts of rooms or hallways. All that is indicated is that each grid area provides the most appropriate area on which to work in order to strengthen a particular life energy.
- The *ba gua* map does not assume that you have to match the function of the area of the dwelling with that indicated by the map. Thus, there is no necessity to put your home office in the career section or your main bedroom in the relationship area (though there is useful energy reinforcement if this happens). Rather, put your energy enhancements in the appropriate areas

200

of the house. If, therefore, the lounge room is in your relationship area, you might place in it family pictures or mementos of occasions significant to your relationships (see Chapter 4).

- The *ba gua* map and associated energy enhancements can be applied to a room, table or desk in the same manner as to a whole dwelling. In the case of a room, you must again locate the main energetic entry point and align from this doorway; in the case of a desk, the edge of the desk where you sit is the 'front' side of the *ba gua*. (Interestingly, Feng Shui does not recommend a desk be square — a standard rectangular shape is quite satisfactory.)

  'Room' *ba gua* is often practised to supplement 'dwelling' *ba gua* when part of the dwelling is missing (when the map covers empty space). It is also useful in work situations, where the controllable amount of local environment can be very limited. Thus, *ba gua* can be applied at work, in an office, cubicle or desk.

The significance of areas of the dwelling that extend from or are 'missing' from the *ba gua* map

When the map covers areas of empty space, you may need to reinforce the life energy areas that contain them. The more empty space in one area of the map, the more significant the energy reinforcement will need to be. This is where you could practise 'room' *ba gua*, using a *ba gua* map of the room, to reinforce the energy that may be deficient.

Areas of the dwelling that extend outside the *ba gua* map create a yang condition in that area. This can be useful but should not be overdone. Building a 20-metre-long extension onto the wealth area of a house will also extend the size of the *ba gua* map, actually creating more areas of space (or deficiency) in other life energy areas. The chance of getting the 'click' will thus be reduced, rather than enhanced.

Squares and directions

Why do we use a grid of squares to fit the eight directions, and what is the meaning of the central square? The nine-square method gives a reasonably accurate picture of where the eight energies are, but it is sometimes difficult to understand all the relationships using this method. There is another way of using *ba gua* and dispensing with the squares. We simply use the eight directions method shown below.

This has the advantage of being very easy to fit to any building. The strongest effects are obtained by working close to the axis of the life energy on which you are focusing. The working area still accords with the nine-square method.

Where the building is of irregular shape and the axes are of different lengths, those energies are treated as strengthened where the

Eight directions of *ba gua*

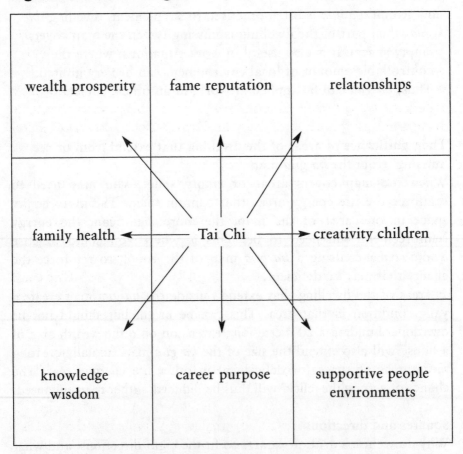

Align the chart over the floor plan of your house so that quadrants 7, 8 and 9 are facing the same direction as your 'front' door.

axis is longer, or weakened where the axis is shorter and dealt with exactly as in the nine-square method.

The central square has disappeared but the energy it represents has not. This is now replaced by the inward direction of the axis. If you want to stabilise any particular life energy, the energy axis is worked on, but worked on close to the centre. Personally, I find this not only the easiest but also the most logical method to use.

Note 9 — Historical development of Feng Shui

One of the greatest problems of newcomers to Feng Shui is sorting out the claims made by the various schools. This is where an understanding of its history can be very useful.

The ideas on which Feng Shui are based, such as chi, yin/yang and the five elements, are very ancient, perhaps over 5000 years old. It is said that the existence of Feng Shui dates back to the trigrams created by Fu Hsi some 2800 years BC, reputedly inspired by his study of the markings on a tortoise shell. I have no problem with this being recognised as the beginning of the ideas which grew into modern Feng Shui. However, I take issue with the claim that the art sprang into being fully formed 5000 years ago.

This assertion is probably based on the old folklore that the *Tseh-king* (the 'Canon of the Dwellings') was written by the legendary emperor Huang Ti. It was, however, the habit of Chinese writers to ascribe their work to more ancient sages (one reason being the supposed 'humility' of the writer, who saw himself as simply transcribing ideas passed down through the generations). One could equally argue that attaching a sage's name to the writings gave them great authority; so the author was less likely to be questioned about the reasoning underlying the writings.

The oldest writing containing Feng Shui principles, of which we can more confidently identify the real author and date, is the *Zhang Shu* (Book of Internment) by Guo Pu. This was written some time in the Jin dynasty (276–420 AD). However, it is not until the tenth century AD that we can identify Feng Shui being practised as a distinct profession. Such practitioners were known as *Xiansheng*.

Feng Shui originally appears to have been more concerned with the dead, in terms of rituals for the placement of bodies and the siting of graves. This branch of Feng Shui, known as Yin Feng Shui, is now considered relatively unimportant to the Feng Shui of the living. Yin Feng Shui grew from the principle of ancestor worship. Obviously, the ancestors' power and willingness to interfere favourably in the affairs of the living would be influenced by the Feng Shui of their grave sites (the 'dwelling' of the spirit).

The grave site was one place where compass directions started to assume importance. Long before Feng Shui ever became formalised, Confucius had stated that the dead should be buried with their heads facing north. (This related to the yin principle associated with death and decomposition). As a natural consequence, it then became very inauspicious for the living to sleep with the head facing north or to have the 'head' of their building facing that direction.

As far as the Feng Shui of the living was concerned, a number of schools of thought developed. The earlier schools can be called the landform schools. The *Xiansheng* would look at the mountains, hills, rivers and lakes and see these as expressions of the underlying chi in the area, which they could then interpret. Of course, there are some areas of land, such as plains, which have few geographical features and other techniques evolved to measure energy there.

The Feng Shui compass, or *Luopan*, was developed to provide the information from which the *Xiansheng* could form their energy assessments. There was also an increased understanding that the energy of the occupant was important as well, which led to the development of the schools using stars, elements and personal numbers. The philosophy was developing that buildings could be likened to living organisms and that energy flows within buildings should conform to those found in actual living organisms.

In other words, Feng Shui has always been a living, growing art, not a one-time mystical revelation. Each school of Feng Shui uses different tools but all have the same objective — to understand the energy in the environment and make it work better for the individual living there. In this sense, the Feng Shui I practise, and which underlies the positive Feng Shui approach, is unashamedly eclectic. It picks the best tools from the different schools, and seeks to refine and improve itself continually, in accordance with the results of Feng Shui research and our increasing scientific understanding of environmental chi and personal chi and of how these interact.

Note 10 — The internal chi environment

People are simply part of the natural world and it should come as no surprise that, just as the natural world has flows of chi within it, so do human beings. Because human beings are usually of intense interest to other human beings, we know far more about chi flows within the human body than we do about those within the environment.

Basically the sources of chi for human beings are:
- air;
- food;
- water; and
- environment.

Once obtained, chi is circulated around the human body in a system of channels. It is used in physical, mental, emotional and spiritual activities. Just as we take in raw products and transform them into products useful to the body, we do so with chi. Thus, you will hear references to *shen* (emotional energy) and *yi* (mental energy). There are also many classifications of chi as it is used in various metabolic processes.

We tend to think of our waste products with distaste but they are all part of a finely balanced ecosystem. Plants would die without the waste carbon dioxide from the respiration of animals, and other waste products are endlessly recycled.

Thus, although chi flows through us and back into the environment, this does not mean that we should not practise a little personal waste management! Chi associated with negative emotions has negative effects on our neighbours (and ourselves). The more we can eliminate negative emotions, the better our overall environmental energy will be.

Note 11 — Geopathic stress and earth rays

You may have seen reference to geopathic stress and negative earth rays. Geopathic stress occurs when the background geomagnetic energy moves out of the beneficial range for human beings because of some natural or artificial occurrence. This can all sound rather alarming and mysterious, but geopathic stress is no more mysterious than chi energy becoming a little more yin or yang than is good for us. Natural occurrences that can result in geopathic stress include geological faults, large bodies of metal ores and underground water. Artificial occurrences arise from such things as underground drains, sewers, pipes, cables and transmission lines. Underground road and rail tunnels can also cause significant impact, as can underground mining operations. Earth rays are simply the name given to the wavelengths that emanate from such a field.

What can we do about such things? If you know that a property is built on an active fault line, an area of geological instability, or over a mine or cavern then it probably makes sense to avoid such areas. You probably would anyway, even if you knew nothing about Feng Shui. On the other hand, if things seem to be going along all right, I would not worry too much. We could worry ourselves about a meteorite landing on earth, a virulent new plague or the poles of the earth suddenly tilting; however, we get through life without fussing too much over these risks, so we can probably manage to live with the risk of some unknown geologic instability suddenly manifesting beneath our feet!

You might come across a claim that 'research' has been done showing that everyone who dies of cancer has lived in a house subject to 'negative' earth rays. This research conveniently ignores the fact that most occupants of the same houses have lived to a ripe old age and that people move from house to house anyway.

If you believe this research, everyone who has contracted lung cancer from smoking, or skin cancer from overexposure to the sun, also has chosen to live in houses subject to negative earth rays. What you breathe, your diet, your exposure to chemical carcinogens and time you spend unprotected out in the sun are going to have much more effect on any risk of cancer you may carry.

Note 12 — Ghosts

As outlined in Note 9, one of the original major branches of Feng Shui, Yin Feng Shui, dealt with maintaining the energetic health of departed ancestors (what we in the West might refer to as ghosts). In general, this meant maintaining the appropriate burial site for the ancestor, keeping them strong and well-disposed towards their descendants. However, the Chinese, like those of other cultures, also identified some environments that were haunted (whether by one's own ancestors or by others). Inevitably, some Feng Shui consultants were called in to assist in these 'environmental' problems, and developed skills in this area which are rather specialised.

As well as problems with ghosts, the Chinese identified problems with more elemental energies, and developed various techniques which often go under the heading of 'space clearing' (though this may sometimes mean simply the clearing of stagnant energy). While the positive Feng Shui program deals with stagnant energy, it does not deal with energies relating to ghosts or other elemental energies; if you have problems in this area you should seek more specialised advice.

Note 13 — When to use a Feng Shui consultant

Use a Feng Shui consultant as you would a doctor — when you are sick, have a problem or are in need of a check-up. In Feng Shui terms, you might be embarking on a major new activity or taking on an important acquisition, and want to be sure your environmental energy can support the new activity or that the acquisition will support your lifestyle energetically.

The doctor analogy is useful because it brings home the fact that, in the case of physical health, it is nutrition and exercise that play the major roles in determining long-term health. We, not our doctors, have to assume responsibility for these. (However, when we are sick, it is right and proper we go to the doctor, and neither does the occasional check-up hurt.) Apply the same logic to Feng Shui. Assume responsibility for maintaining your own environment and you may never need to call in the experts.

It makes sense to use a consultant when buying a house or business premises. Nine-hundred and ninety-nine out of every 1000 Feng Shui problems are relatively easy and cheap to fix; however, when you are spending a couple of hundred thousand dollars or more, the relative cost of a consultant is such a small fraction of the total cost of discovering a big Feng Shui problem that it seems only prudent to have expert advice. Think of it as you would getting a pest inspection!

You could also go to an expert every time you redecorated, bought some new furniture or there was some change in your local environment. However, most of us could not afford this, just as most of us cannot afford to retain our own personal health consultant to advise on every meal we have and movement that we make; we seem to get through life making a few wrong decisions and learning by them. This is where the positive Feng Shui program comes in, to enable you to take a sensible approach to your day-to-day Feng Shui decisions, lessen your mistakes and identify opportunities that you might otherwise not have thought of.

Note 14 — Fortune tables

One technique used in Feng Shui is to combine the concepts of strengthening energy through the use of symbols and the relationship of the eight major life energies of the *ba gua* by using a 'fortune table'.

In this technique a square table is set aside for Feng Shui purposes. The *ba gua* map is then placed over the table to identify the areas of the table associated with each of the eight major life energies. An appropriate symbol for each of the energies is then placed in each square. (The 'front' of the table is the side at which you approach the table. That is where you stand when placing the symbols on the table.)

To increase energy you might cover the table in a red or gold tablecloth. The table can be placed anywhere but should ideally be in a bright, well-ventilated area where it is easily visible.

Note 15 — Using crystals

Next to mirrors, crystals are probably the most well-known Feng Shui cure. Most of us probably think we know what a crystal is but in fact it is any substance with an ordered internal structure, whether or not this reflects itself in smooth plane surfaces. Crystals can have amazing power and our technology has found many uses for them, from the humble crystal radio to quartz watches and highly sophisticated satellite communications, laser and computer technology.

Simply applying pressure to a quartz rock crystal will cause it to develop an electrical charge, a phenomenon known as piezo-electricity. Light entering a crystal is refracted, or bent. Some crystals absorb short wavelengths, such as ultraviolet light or X-rays, and then emit them in longer visible wavelengths, a property known as fluorescence. Some crystals hold on to these energies and only later release them as phosphorescence.

Most Feng Shui crystals sold in shops are clear, round, multifaceted and made from lead glass. These crystals are used to balance chi by distributing it to all areas of a room. Where the chi is strong, such a crystal will scatter it in all directions. This same design of crystal also assists in a situation where the chi is thick and slow moving. Note that this type of crystal does not generate energy but simply refracts it and will only work where there is a good light source.

The same crystal can be used to balance *ba gua* imbalances caused by irregular shapes of a room or dwelling. (Note: to do this they must be placed opposite a window. If there is no suitable window, the imbalance should be corrected by use of a mirror (see Note 18) or a quartz crystal, which generates as well as disperses energy.)

Much of the Feng Shui use of crystals stops at remedying energy deficiencies of buildings. This is a pity, as the only reason we are remedying these deficiencies is the impact that they have on the occupants. We should also focus on the direct energy effects that crystals can have on a person. For instance, coloured crystals are used in chromotherapy (using colours to heal) and colour acupuncture (a more specialised form of chromotherapy where different frequencies of laser light are used to stimulate acupoints and achieve particular effects). Many people wear or carry a crystal in their pocket for the increased energy and concentration that it gives them.

The darker and more opaque a crystal, the more it will strengthen yin; the lighter, more brilliant and more sparkling a crystal, the more it will strengthen yang.

Rock crystal is another name for clear quartz (silicon dioxide). Quartz is quite often coloured by impurities. For instance, yellow beach sand is quartz stained by iron. Other varieties of quartz include amethyst (purple), rose quartz (pink), citrine (yellow) and smoky quartz (black). The colours affect the five elements energy nature of crystal.

Cutglass crystals represent the water element and can be used to counterbalance fire energy, as in a window with excessive exposure to sunlight.

Note 16 — Symbolic meanings of plants

PLANT	SYMBOLIC MEANING
Apple	Peace and prosperity
Azalea	Feminine grace
Bamboo	Long life and youth
Cherry tree	Feminine beauty
Chrysanthemum	Nobility
Cypress	Joyousness and long life
Jasmine	Sweetness, friendship and love
Lotus	Fruitfulness
Magnolia	Feminine sweetness
Mulberry	Domestic peace, good fortune, rejuvenation
Narcissus oak	Masculine strength and virility
Oleander	Beauty
Orange	Happiness and prosperity
Orchids	Love, beauty, fertility, strength and gracefulness
Peach	Friendship, marriage and immortality
Pear	Purity and long life
Peony (Mu Dan)	The Queen of Flowers — the flower of wealth, honour and distinction. White peony symbolises women distinguished as much by their wit as their beauty. The peony is one of the flowers of the four seasons (spring).
Persimmon	Generally means matters or affairs. When combined with the lily and miraculous mushroom, it means 'May everything proceed as you wish.' As a tree it has four virtues — it has long life, it provides shade and shelter for birds and it harbours no vermin.
Pine	Long life
Plum blossom	Long life, youth, beauty and unconquerable spirit
Pomegranate	Many prosperous offspring
Rose	Beauty and love
Tangerine	Prosperity
Willow	Gentleness and feminine grace

Note 17 — Designing 'colour schemes'

There are four basic considerations when designing an appropriate colour scheme:

1 Is the nature of the size, construction and climate of the room yin or yang?
2 Is the nature of the function of the room yin or yang?
3 Does the room's occupant have any special requirements on a yin/yang basis?
4 What are the favourite colours of the room's occupant?

1 Is the nature of the size, construction and climate of the room yin or yang?

The yin/yang nature of a room can be judged as follows:

• If the room is very small, dark, has a cool temperature or tends to be quiet, damp and moist, then the chi of that room will be yin in nature.
• If the room is very large, brightly lit, has a warm temperature or tends to be draughty, dry and filled with noise, then the chi of that room would be yang in nature.

Obviously most rooms will be a mixture of the above characteristics. The more difficult it is to make up your mind about whether the room is yin or yang, the more balanced the nature of that room will tend to be.

Standard practice would be to try to eliminate any sha chi (excess yang), si chi (excess yin) by using opposing yin/yang colours — particularly if the yin/yang state was not appropriate to the function of the room (see below).

Where a room is in an area of the house that is outside the 'square' of the house, it may need to be a little more yin. Where a room is adjacent to an area missing from the 'square', it may need to be made a little more yang (see Note 8).

2 Is the nature of the function of the room yin or yang?

Rooms that are yang by the nature of their function include the living room, kitchen, dining room, family room, playroom, home office, study (if creative work is done there), hobby room, exercise room, hall, foyer and computer room.

Rooms that are yin by the nature of their function include the bedroom, bathroom, laundry, pantry, storeroom, garage, study (if learning and growth take place there) and rooms for passive entertainment (for example, watching television or listening to music).

The colours should reflect the nature of the room, supporting the activity that takes place there.

3 Does the room's occupant have any special requirements on a yin/yang basis?

This relates to the personal energy objectives of the person occupying that room.

4 What are the favourite colours of the room's occupant?

As well as their general effect, colours can have effects specific to a person. Consider using these colours in the areas of the dwelling that are 'personal' to you or to the person you are thinking of. To determine the colours that have most impact, ask yourself (or them) the following questions:

- Which colour do you find the most pleasing?
  This choice should have remained consistent over a long period of time and is reflected in the colour most often chosen when decorating, the colour of your clothes, and of your furniture and ornaments. It is referred to as your 'soul colour'. Use in any of your personal areas.
- Which colour do you find the most relaxing?
  This is your healing colour. Use in your bedroom.
- Which colour do you find most inspirational?
  Use it in your study, or any area where most of your thinking and planning is done.

The five elements' colours and their energetic impact

Water — black/ebony/navy blue

True black is when all light waves are absorbed and non-reflected, and this is not encountered very often in nature. What we perceive as black are the very short, high-frequency waves from navy blue to violet as it moves out of the visible spectrum into ultraviolet.

This is seen as a cooling, cleansing energy. You may find it contradictory that we worry about getting sunburn from a cooling energy like ultraviolet, but remember, you can get 'burnt' from very cold ice. Many flowers emit ultraviolet light, which is one way to have this energy in your home without hazard.

Mix black paints yourself to ensure they contain dark blue, violet or indigo, as black would in nature. Pure black is a very draining energy — it is an absence of colour rather than very short-frequency colour. There is no black in the spectrum.

Water colour facts:
- symbolic meaning — the blessings of heaven;
- seen as cool — yin; and
- harmonious with white and/or green.

Water effects of hues, tints and shades:
- Blue lowers rate of breathing and blood pressure, makes us feel cooler and turns us inward mentally.
- Blue encourages slowing down, higher self-esteem, ecstasy, relaxation and spirituality.
- Blue discourages conversation, optimism, eating, feeling energised and insecurity.
- Deep blue stimulates the pituitary gland and helps regulate sleep patterns.
- Dark blue has pain-healing properties and helps keep bone marrow healthy.
- Light and soft blue make us feel quiet and protected; blue inspires mental control, clarity and creativity; midnight blue has a strong sedative effect; too much dark blue can be depressing.

Earth — yellow/gold/tan
The colour yellow is around the middle of the spectrum and is the most visible of colours (note its use in road signs and markings, as well as in safety clothes).

Earth colour facts:
- symbolic meaning — centre and royalty;
- colour seen as dense — yang;
- harmonious with red and/or white; and
- earth colours include brown, tan, pink and beige. Many wood colours are earth colours.

Earth effects of hues, tints and shades:
- Yellow encourages clarity, abundance, illumination, good judgment, good organisation and self-confidence; aids powers of discernment when associated with the intellectual side of the mind; helps memory, clear thinking and decision-making.
- Yellow discourages egocentricity, isolation and inactivity.
- Yellow stimulates the brain, making you alert, clear-headed and decisive.
- Yellow strengthens the nervous system, activates the lymph system and cleanses the digestive tract. Works well on the pancreas, liver and gall bladder.
- Apricot or peach is good for nervous exhaustion.
- Orange frees and releases emotions. It lifts the spirits.

Wood — green/jade/blue greens
Green lies on the yin side of the spectrum, from yellow. The more yellow the green, the more yang; the more blue the green, the more yin. In general, green works better when it is bright and has evenly balanced mixes of blue and yellow. Green encourages growth, tranquillity and awakening. We instinctively seek green when under stress.
   Wood colour facts:
- symbolic meaning — long life, peace;
- colour seen as lively, yin; and
- harmonious with blue and/or red.

Wood effects of hues, tints and shades:
- Green works to create physical equilibrium and relaxation. Stimulates pituitary gland and sympathetic nervous system, relaxing muscles and encouraging deep breathing.
- Dark green soothes the emotions.
- Muddy, dull or olive green indicates decay.
- Lime and olive green can have a detrimental effect on physical and emotional health as associated with envy, resentment and possessiveness.
- Green can be cold or warm, depending on the proportion of blue and yellow in it.
- Green discourages internal focus, control, generosity.

Metal — white/ivory/silver

The colour white is actually a mix of all the colours. These can be separated out of white light by using a prism (rain acts as a natural prism to create the rainbow effect). White light is hueless but it may have a considerable colour range, particularly in the yellow/blue direction. It is reflective, hence its association with metal colours.

Metal colour facts:
- symbolic meaning — purity;
- colour seen as bright, yang; and
- harmonious with yellow and/or blue.

Metal effects of hues, tint and shades:
- White provides all-round colour of protection, brings peace and comfort, alleviates emotional shock and despair. Too much white can be cold and isolating, creating separateness.
- Bluish-white is very cold and isolating.
- Peachy, yellowy, creamy whites are warmer.

Fire — red, purple

Fire colour has the longest wavelength and the slowest vibratory rate.

Fire colour facts:
- symbolic meaning — joy, fame and luck;
- colour seen as warm, yang; and
- harmonious with green and or yellow/gold.

Fire effects of hues, tints and shades:
- Red raises blood pressure, stimulates the adrenal glands as well as the lower or sex energy chakra.
- Red is related to vitality, ambition, irritation, and anger.
- Red encourages energy, excitement, warmth.
- Red discourages contemplation, inward and outward focus, depression.
- Pink stimulates the heart chakra.
- Pink, rose or peach colours create loving feelings.
- Pink is associated with the feminine.

Note 18 — Using mirrors

Mirrors include any object that reflects images, for example, metal surfaces and highly polished furniture. A fair amount of Feng Shui mirror folklore has grown up, some of which is not always accurate. An interesting way to understand how mirrors should and should not be used is to explore some of the statements of this folklore.

Mirrors should always reflect something pleasant. Not totally true. What you should ensure is that unpleasant images in mirrors are not visible to those inside the dwelling.

Mirrors should not distort or cut into the image of a person. Not really true. There would be few mirrors, or positions in which you could place mirrors, where you could always be sure that the full body of a person would be reflected from all positions you can see the mirror.

There is, however, a bad psychological message from positioning mirrors that show the body but not the head. Certainly it would not be a good idea to have a crack in the mirror that ran through the image. Mirror tiles are sometimes not recommended because the image is split over several tiles, representing separation of chi, but you do not need to worry about this. Water reflections by their nature 'distort' images but such moving distortions are no problem. It is if a mirror permanently shows your image in a distorted way that you should change it.

Mirrors should always have frames to contain the chi of the image. Pure folklore; natural reflections are not framed. You can, however, use a frame to highlight the mirror image. This would be a good idea if you have a very pleasant scene reflected in the mirror, as it would strengthen the effect of it. If all you see in the mirror is yourself, a frame helps those who like to admire themselves!

Mirrors should not be hung opposite a door or window since they reflect the chi out and prevent it flowing round the home. Not really true. For a start, if you have an unpleasant site opposite your front door or window you might want to reflect the image back out of the house. The important thing here is that the unpleasant image is not visible to people in the house; if it is, you have only strengthened the bad influence.

Unfortunately, a lot of Feng Shui mirror advice seems ignorant of basic physics. Mirrors do not contain images, they reflect them. Depending on where you stand in front of a mirror, the image will be different, so that what you see is a reflection unique to your own position: angle of incidence = angle of reflection. If you stand right in front, your image is opposite you; if you are to one side, what you see is the image from the opposite side. A well-positioned mirror can thus do numerous things at the same time, such as reflecting bad images out and spreading good images to different corners of the dwelling.

Mirrors can make it difficult to sleep in a bedroom. Quite true. The more mirror area in a bedroom, the more chi energy will be moved around the room. If when in bed you can see yourself in a mirror, the energy is being moved in your direction and will be particularly disturbing. Mirrored doors on wardrobes have huge areas of reflection and can be particularly disturbing.

Mirrors should not face each other. True. The reflection of energy backwards and forwards creates excess chi.

Mirrors should be placed in 'dead', stagnant areas of the house. True. The stirring up of energy that we would find disturbing in the bedroom has a useful effect in turning stagnant chi into sheng (beneficial) chi.

Mirrors can slow chi down in halls and corridors. True — although, admittedly, this seems contradictory when we have just said that mirrors can stir up energy. Long, narrow corridors and halls speed up the flow of chi. If this chi is reflected back into its own flow then the chi is slowed. Slowing chi by opposing flows is a standard technique in chi acupressure/massage and meditation.

If mirrors are placed on the walls that are next to missing areas, they can help reinforce the energy of these areas.

More mirror information
Ba gua *mirrors*
These are mirrors surrounded by the *ba gua* symbols; they are 'yin' mirrors and should never be hung inside a dwelling. (See Notes 7 and 8 for more information on the *ba gua*.) You will sometimes see convex and concave mirrors.

- Convex mirrors: These disperse light and are good for reflecting away energies we do not want.
- Concave mirrors: These draw light to a focal point before dispersing it beyond this point. If you have a negative image you can concentrate this at one point and use a Feng Shui cure there to transform the energy. Warning: Anything between the mirror and the focal point is in for a very concentrated blast of negative energy! For ordinary use, it is better to focus positive energy, in an area such as a desk or in a creative environment. (Note: Be *sure* you are focusing positive energy.)

Five elements placement of mirrors
A mirror's best position is on the dragon (left-hand side) wall of a room or house. Avoid placing on the tiger (right-hand side) or turtle side (rear wall). At desks, when your back is unprotected, place mirrors in which you can see people approaching your desk on your left side.

Note 19 — Managing mobile phones, waterbeds and electric blankets

These are all items where we need to consider management of exposure to electromagnetic radiation. While there are still many studies taking place of the impact of mobile phones on health, I suspect that as an isolated item they will not present a significant problem in themselves. What concerns me is the total electromagnetic environment and its overall impact. (Is anyone researching the effect of answering our mobile phone while lying in our electrically heated waterbed watching TV with the digital electric clock next to our head and the power-box behind the wall at the head of the bed?) The more we can do to minimise exposure, the better. Therefore try to keep the frequency and duration of phone calls on a mobile to a minimum. Use other phones where you can. Forget using an earpiece — as this book goes to press, research indicates that the cord acts as an aerial that increases exposure of the head.

Put electric blankets on before you go to bed then turn them off when you sleep.

Waterbeds are generally not so bad, having their heating element at the foot of the bed and only being in operation when they fall below thermostat set level. One trick is to raise the thermostat level when you get out of bed and lower it when you get in. This means the bed is toasty warm when you get in but will not fall below the thermostat level for quite a few hours, ensuring no EMR exposure during this period.

Contacts

Australia

Feng Shui Academy
www.livingchi.com.au

STATE OFFICES

New South Wales (National
  Head Office)
PO Box 1020
Burwood North NSW 2134
Tel/Fax: (02) 9797 9355

Queensland
PO Box 2475
BC Qld 4006
Tel: (07) 3358 1955

South Australia
GPO Box 1306
Adelaide SA 5001
Tel: (08) 8287 3571

Queensland
Bundaberg (07) 4153 4428
Gold Coast (07) 5572 8921
Gympie (07) 5486 5131
Rockhampton (07) 4939 5845
Sunshine Coast (07) 5491 2314
Toowoomba (07) 4636 5034

Tasmania
PO Box 1688
Launceston TAS 7250
Tel: (03) 6362 3428

REGIONAL OFFICES

New South Wales
Albury/Corowra (02) 6033 3172
Baradine (02) 6843 1982
Central Coast (02) 4332 7176
Coonabarabran (02) 6842 2079
Kootingal (02) 6765 8292
Newcastle (02) 4942 2951
Orange (02) 6365 8309
Tamworth (02) 6765 8292
Woollongong (02) 4261 5786

Index

acupressure, 32, 85, 181
acupuncture, 13, 85
advertisements, 19, 20
aeroplanes, 25
animals, 84
aroma energy, 85–6, 148–51
astronauts, 27–8

ba gua, 84
    diagrams, 192–3
    eight directions of, 202
    eight major life areas, 184, 194–202
    fortune tables, 208
    literal translation, 192
    map, 196–203
    mirrors, 218
    modern development, 184
bathrooms, 172–3
bedrooms, 75, 167, 167–171
bio-energy, 83–5, 144–7
birth element, 87
bonsai plants, 174
breathing, chi, 180–1
building component, 63, 69–70
buildings, 165–7
buildings, local, 159–161
business premises, 23–25, 56–7, 189

career (purpose), 51, 52, 195
chi, 16
    chi kung, 180
    classifications, 205
    cycle of change, 35
    diet, 181
    energy, 18, 32–34
    exercises, 181
    frequencies, 39–40
    harmonisation, 33
    internal chi environment, 205–206
    interrelationship of Feng Shui, 181–2
    'life energy', 33
    quality of, 34, 38–9
    sha chi, 37–8
    sheng chi, 38
    si chi, 36–7
    stagnant chi, 38
    terminology, 36
    universal, 27
    vibrations, 39–40
    wu chi, 43
children (creativity), 51, 55, 195
climate, local area, 152–3
clocks, 173–4
colour, 74, 102, 105, 107
    designing colour schemes, 211–16
compass directions, 182–184
computers, electromagnetic
    radiation, 75
consultants, 207–208
creation, 44, 45
creativity, 12, 51, 55
creativity (children), 51, 55, 195
crystallised energy, 79–81, 122–36
crystals, 111–13, 209–210

destiny, 10
diet, chi, 181
dining rooms, 172
directions, 188
dragons, 12
dragon veins, 42
dried flower arrangements, 174–5

earth
    colours, 214
    earth nature energy, 86, 88, 93
    rays, 206–207
El Nino, 40–1
electric blankets, 219–20
electromagnetic energy, 73–6, 99–115
electromagnetic radiation, 33, 75–6,
    107–109

energy
    different directions, 185
    eight energy conditions, 72
    energetic ocean, 17, 32
    environment as, 11, 16
    identifying individual's needs, 11
    quality of, 17
    vibration, 39
    what is, 17–18
energy phases, 86–93
environment
    building picture of, 61
    collecting information about, 61
    energy, as, 11, 16
    harmonising with, 7
    image of, 21
    modifying, 11
    positive approach to, 21
    selection of, 10
    significant, identification of, 62, 94
    typical environments, 62
    Western 'matter'-orientated view, 16, 17
environmental energy profile, 61, 62, 94
exercises, chi, 191

family, 53, 56, 189, 195
Feng Shui
    approaches to, 13–14
    'bad', 28
    benefits, 18
    Chinese ideograms for, 11
    common questions about, 23–30
    enhancements, impact of, 190
    essence of, 11
    ethical issues, 30
    getting most out of program, 22
    historical development, 183, 203–205
    objectives, 13, 19
    positive Feng Shui program, 18–21
    reasons to practise, 9
    skill development, 179
    spectrum of techniques, 13–14
    techniques, 13, 14
    traditional Chinese perspective, 16
    'used up', 26–7
    what is, 7, 10
fire, 86, 92, 214

fixtures, 63, 71–2, 173
fortune tables, 208
frequency, 30, 39
Fu Hsi, 192, 203
furnishings, 63, 71–2, 173

garages, 173
geopathic stress, 206–207
ghosts, 207
gravity, 33, 89
Guo Pu, 204

happiness, 9–11, 19
health, 12, 19, 51, 53, 195
helpful people (travel), 51, 55, 195
hills, 156–7
home environment components, 63
home office, 173
houses
    ba gua map, 196–203
    business premises and, 24
    energetic activities, 167–75
    ownership, 23
    split-level, 165
Huang Ti, 203

I Ching, 192–3

King Wen, 193
kitchens, 171–2

lakes, 157
land, 63, 67–8, 163–5
landforms, local, 153, 154–5, 158
Lao Tse, 43
life activities, harmonising, 189
life energy centres, 51
light, 73, 74, 100–102
living rooms, 172
local area, 63, 65–6, 151–61
longevity, statue, 10
luck, 10
luopan, 183, 204

Maslow, A.H., 53, 54
massage, 181
meditation, 181
metal nature energy, 86, 92
mirrors, 110–11, 216–18
mobile phones, 219–20
moisture energy, 82–3, 140–3

mountains, 156–7
movement energy, 78, 119–22
music, 77
myths about Feng Shui, 22–3

nutrition, chi, 181

occupants' Feng Shui, 56–7, 189
oceans, 157

personal energy profile, 31, 177
    chi conditions, adjusting, 176
    determining approach, 49–50
    Form 1, 59
    life energy centres, 55–6
    monitoring changes in personal
        energy, 56
    objectives, identifying, 58
    yin and yang, 48–9
personal growth (education), 51, 52
personal numbers, 57, 191
pets, 84–5
physical objects crystallised energy,
    79–81
plants, symbolic meanings, 210–11
positive approach, 18–21
productivity, improving, 12
property, 23
prosperity, 53–4, 195

relationships, 12, 51, 54, 170, 195
reputation (fame), 51, 54, 195
rivers, 157
roads, 162
rooms
    ba gua map, 196–203
    designing colour schemes, 211–16
    energetic nature of activities, 167–73
    home environment, 63, 70–1

science, 14–15, 33
Seasonally Affective Disorder (SAD), 100
second-hand goods, 28
self-actualisation, 53
sharp objects, 80
shen, 205
sleep, 167–69
soil types, 158
sound energy, 76–8, 115–19
Southern Oscillation Index, 40

Space Station Freedom, 27
stars, 28, 57, 191
stone columns, 175
storerooms, 173
straight lines, 80
streams, 157
subconscious, 19, 20
superstition, 15

Tai Chi, 181, 195
taste, 86
tents, 25
thermal energy, 81–2, 136–9
time, 28
travel, 51, 55
Tseh-king, 203

universe, 28, 33, 90
    wu chi, 43

vegetation, 159
visual arts, 74, 113–15

water
    colours, 213
    symbolism, 11
    water cycle, 34–5
    water nature energy, 86, 93
waterbeds, 219–20
waves, 90
wealth, 9, 10, 51, 53–4, 195
wind, symbolism, 11
wisdom, 51, 195
wood, 86, 92, 214

Xiansheng, 204

yi, 205
yin and yang, 42–9
    conditions of chi, 35
    creation, 44
    definition, 42
    directions, 46
    energy relationships, 48
    five elemental energy phases, 90–1
    imbalance, 48–9
    physical objects, 79
Yin Feng Shui, 204

Zhang Shu, 204